commodities initially endowed upon each individual by the experimenter. The utility functions and technology are inherently unobservable; however, their consequences are observable. In a market experiment, the reduced form of the environment is given by the supply and demand schedules, which summarize the incentives to exchange.

Elements of an institution include a language (comprised of messages sent by each participant), allocation rules, cost imputation rules, and adjustment process rules.[9] All components of an institution, which define each agent's property rights in communication and in exchange, are observable. An institution is given in the laboratory by the experimental instructions, which describe the rules of exchange that each participant receives. One example of a familiar institution is the English (or progressive) auction, commonly used to sell objects (*e.g.*, art or livestock) in art/antique auction houses or at county fairs. Bidders in an English auction must improve upon (*i.e.*, bid higher than) the standing bid in order for their bid (message) to be recognized by the seller. The last bidder, the one who bids the highest, is allocated the object and pays the seller the amount of the final bid.

Once an environment and institution are established in the laboratory, the third major element of a microeconomic system, behavior, can be observed. The resulting behavior of participants in an experiment is a function of both the environment and the institution. *Behavior is not induced*, the incentives that participants face are.[10]

---

[9] Messages, for example, might include a bid or an offer, or acceptance of a bid or an offer. The allocation rule is a function of the messages of all participants, and specifies the allocation of commodities. The cost imputation rule gives the monetary payment each agent receives as a result of the messages. Adjustment process rules simply define the starting, transition, and stopping rules of the experiment.

[10] If behavior were induced, experimentation would be synonymous with simulation, in which behavior is assumed and some element of randomness is injected into the process. For instance, participants in a Cournot (quantity-setting market) institution are not constrained to choose the Cournot quantities. Rather, each participant selects a quantity from his choice set, which includes the Cournot quantity among several other production alternatives.

A laboratory microeconomic system is created by *inducing value*, which involves assigning monetary value to units of experimental assets.[11] For instance, each seller in a laboratory market is assigned a cost for each unit of a commodity that he might choose to sell. The difference between the price at which he sells a unit and its cost, determines the seller's profit from the sale of that unit. Likewise, each buyer is given the redemption value, guaranteed by the experimenter, associated with each unit of the commodity that he might choose to purchase. The difference between the resale (redemption) value of a unit and the price he pays for the unit, determines the profit that the buyer earns on the unit. In this manner, the monetary value of a decision becomes well defined for each market participant.

Control of preferences in a laboratory microeconomic system requires that four precepts are satisfied:

(1) *Nonsatiation*. Utility increases in cash rewards (*i.e.*, each participant prefers more money to less).

(2) *Saliency*. Rewards properly reflect incentives, rewards increase (decrease) in the favorable (unfavorable) outcomes.

(3) *Dominance*. Rewards sufficiently compensate each market participant for any subjective costs associated with participation in the experiment.[12]

(4) *Privacy*. Each participant receives information on his own reward schedule, but not the reward schedules of the other participants.

---

[11] *See* Smith (1976b) for the theory of induced value.

[12] Failing to satisfy dominance could lead to participants making their decisions in a purely random fashion, because the monetary compensation does not sufficiently compensate them for their decision costs. Many experiments have been run in which payoffs have been doubled, tripled, or even more. In general, these increases do not significantly affect the mean of observed participant behavior. As long as participants earn at least the opportunity cost of their time, the results are not significantly affected. Smith and Walker (1993) report that increasing the payouts usually does not change the mean of the data, although it generally reduces the variance of the observations about their mean.

Precepts (1) through (4) permit tests of theory. However, an additional precept is necessary for addressing whether replicable laboratory results shed light on the behavior in and performance of naturally-occurring markets:

(5) *Parallelism.* Hypotheses that are supported in one laboratory or field market experiment also hold in other laboratory or field markets when corresponding conditions are held constant.

Like theory, laboratory markets may or may not parallel the forces that drive naturally-occurring markets. Of course, if specific theories or laboratory markets are used to inform policy, it is desirable that they provide a credible parallel. The use of careful experimental design, sometimes enhanced by computerized laboratories, permits the study of fairly sophisticated markets.[13]

The above methodology is usually applied in university laboratories, and laboratory market participants are generally college undergraduates or graduate students, who likely are not as sophisticated as the agents in markets of interest. Hence, the methodological issue arises that laboratory market outcomes might vary with the pool of participants. Most economic theories are based on the concept of rationality, agents maximizing their utility given constraints. When market outcomes differ with the subject pool, this suggests either that rationality is not a generalizable trait (*e.g.*, students are not rational, but OPEC members are), or that experience with a parallel institution in the naturally-occurring economy is important. Participants usually receive training in a specific laboratory institution, especially for the more complex institutions. Laboratory markets of different types have been run with GE executives,[14] Chicago over-the-counter stock traders,[15] Energy Administration officials, natural gas corporation

---

[13] *See*, for instance, the Rassenti, Reynolds, and Smith (1989) study of cotenancy in laboratory networks which are designed to parallel natural gas networks. *See also* Hong and Plott's (1982) telephone market study of rate filing policies for inland water transportation; and Smith (1993), which discusses the laboratory market foundation of the recently formed Arizona Stock Exchange (AZX).

[14] Fouraker and Siegel (1963).

[15] King, Smith, Williams, and Van Boening (*forthcoming*).

7

executives,[16] Eastern European reformers,[17] and other professionals. In general, these groups do *not* exhibit behavior that is significantly different than that of student participants in laboratory markets.[18] Note that if subject pool selection becomes an issue, the laboratory accommodates its analysis.[19,20] Still, in the interest of satisfying payoff dominance while optimizing the research output subject to budget constraints (the opportunity cost of a student participant likely is lower than that of a Chicago Mercantile

---

[16] Smith presented the results of running experiments with both regulators and then with some of the regulated parties when summarizing his research on natural gas networks in Rassenti, Reynolds, and Smith (1989) at the American Enterprise Institute Conference on Policy Approaches to the Deregulation of Network Industries, October 10-11, 1990.

[17] This data was collected by Michael Block and Vernon Smith, both of the University of Arizona, during a World Bank sponsored conference on market reform, Vienna, Austria (September 1992 and July 1993).

[18] *See* Ball and Cech (1993) for a review of subject pool selection in experimental economics. Many psychology experiments involve different subject pools, however, psychology experiments frequently violate the precepts of nonsatiation, saliency, and dominance (usually by not monetarily rewarding laboratory participants for their decisions). Hence, the results from such experiments should be interpreted with caution. *See* Cox and Isaac (1986) and Smith (1991) for a comparison of the laboratory methodologies utilized in economics and psychology. Wilcox (1989 and 1992) and Smith and Walker (1993) evaluate the use of monetary rewards in laboratory markets.

[19] *See*, for instance, Gerety (1987) which finds that undergraduates and prisoners do not exhibit significantly different propensities to conspire when presented with opportunities to do so in sealed offer auctions (markets in which each seller submits an offer to supply a good or service--similar to government procurement) without the threat of antitrust enforcement. However, as Gerety hypothesized *a priori*, when the threat of enforcement was introduced, by means of a random monetary penalty for a violation, the subject pools viewed the threat differently. Namely, the students exhibited risk-aversion, concentrating excessively on the size of the penalty; while the prisoners were risk-seeking, focusing more on the low probability of detection.

[20] Dyer and Kagel (1992) test common value auction theory in the laboratory using students and professional construction contractors as participants. Several contractors requested information about the architect, though not part of the theory or the experiment. This highlights the importance of specialization in the economy. Theory, and thus experimental tests of theory, circumvent the details that agents in the field use to value a contract, object, or right on which they bid. The details are bypassed by reducing value to a certain or probabilistically uncertain vector of numbers. This makes it possible to focus on the market process itself without all the transaction specific "baggage," which in the field is an extremely (and may be seen as *the*) important problem to practitioners. Sometimes this baggage places field professionals at a disadvantage in laboratory markets. *See*, for instance, Burns (1985).

Exchange trader), and because most economics laboratories are located at universities, college students have been and likely will continue to be the preferred subject pool for most cases.[21]

In laboratory studies, as in econometric studies of naturally-occurring markets, it is possible to incorrectly implement the methodology and consequently draw inappropriate inferences. Beyond the basic precepts of good experimental design, discussed above, many other elements must be considered when designing an experiment.[22] A few other design matters will be discussed below in presenting laboratory findings that relate to competition issues.

III. Some Experimental Results

A. Competitive Behavior and Institutional Effects

Laboratories are well-suited to examining straight-forward (and falsifiable) theoretical predictions. For instance, it is often hypothesized that the competitive outcome, where total surplus is maximized at the intersection of the demand and supply schedules, requires many buyers and sellers, as well as perfect information. The competitive equilibrium prediction provides a relatively accurate description of market performance across many laboratory institutions and environments. However, the speed with which competitive equilibrium is reached, the proximity of observations to competitive predictions, and the propensity for cooperative behavior under various conditions varies with the institution. As Smith (1989) highlights, until the 1960s, economic theories remained largely institution free, with outcomes derived from the environment (market structure and agent knowledge) and *ad hoc* assumptions about demand (*e.g.*, perfect demand revelation or "price-taking" by buyers). For instance, the standard competitive

---

[21] In most laboratory markets, each participant has the same degree of familiarity or *experience* with the institution. This, of course, can be controlled if it is important that the market participants have varying degrees of experience with the market.

[22] Methodological issues are discussed throughout the literature. *See*, for example, volumes of *Research in Experimental Economics*, Greenwich, CT: JAI Press, and Davis and Holt (1992).

equilibrium model says nothing about *how* equilibrium is achieved. Without specifying the mechanics of the underlying institution, such as the trading rules, the competitive model merely assumes that convergence will occur.[23] Important early developments in institution-specific theory include Shubik's introduction (1959) of the extensive form game to industrial organization theory; Hurwicz's theory (1960) of mechanisms; and Vickrey's work (1961) on (first-price, Dutch, second-price, and English) auctions. As Shubik notes (1959, p. 183):

> It is foolish to entertain the delusion that the Cournot, Edgeworth, Chamberlinian, or other 'reaction-curve' assumptions are good approximations of non-co-operative behavior in the market *and* that we can leave all aspects of asset and corporate structure safely assumed away in a *ceteris paribus* condition and still come out with a useful theory of oligopoly.
>
> Before we are in a position to examine the detailed meaning of any type of behavioristic assumption or reaction-curve we must be able to describe with reasonable verisimilitude the salient observable features of a market in a dynamic setting. [*Emphasis in original*]

Institution-specific theories, and laboratory tests of "institution-free" theories (like supply and demand) across different institutions, suggest that institutions matter.[24]

Several institutions have been studied in the laboratory. Two of the more important from an antitrust perspective are the *double-auction* and the *posted-offer* institutions.[25]

---

[23] The concept of the Walrasian auctioneer comes to mind. The Walrasian model provides an institutional framework to describe how equilibrium is achieved. However, the abstract concept of employing a fictitious auctioneer raises the issue of whether the model parallels observable features of any institution in the naturally-occurring economy.

[24] The behavioral results from laboratory tests of auctions led to extensions of Vickrey's auction theories. For example, *see* Cox, Roberson, and Smith (1982) and Cox, Dinkin, and Smith (1993). Bargaining theory has also been altered to reflect laboratory results, *see* Bolton (1991). Other examples of theoretical work prompted by experimental results include Friedman (1984, 1991), Wilson (1987), and Easley and Ledyard (1988).

[25] Thousands of double-auctions and posted-offer experiments have been conducted. *See*, for instance, Smith (1962, 1964, 1967, 1976b, 1981a); Plott and Smith (1978); Smith, Williams, Bratton, and Vannoni (1982); Friedman (1984); Isaac, Ramey, and Williams (1984); Ketchum, Smith, and Williams (1984); and Cox and Oaxaca (1990).

1. The Double-Auction Institution

The double-auction, formulated by Smith (1962, 1964), involves buyers who are free to make bids and accept offers, and sellers who are free to make offers and accept bids for units of a homogenous commodity. Trading takes place over several market periods of specified duration. As Smith (1976a) points out, these markets are similar to real estate and over-the-counter securities markets, as no unaccepted bid or offer is binding in a later period unless it is resubmitted. Another version of the double-auction institution imposes an improvement rule, permitting only those bids (offers) that are higher (lower) than the outstanding bid (offer). Under the improvement rule, the double-auction more closely parallels organized exchanges such as the American or New York Stock Exchange, as the traders cannot cancel a bid or offer that they have made that is currently standing as the lowest offer to sell or the highest bid to buy. With or without the improvement rule, the observed outcomes are roughly the same.

During the past decade, the majority of antitrust cases that were challenged or settled by the FTC involved nonretail markets.[26] The double-auction institution also parallels important features of wholesale or nonretail markets, which frequently involve negotiation of contracts.[27] Hong and Plott (1982) find that when an institution involves direct negotiations (telephone-based negotiations are a key feature of some of the markets that they study in the laboratory) the performance of the market appears similar to that of double-auction markets in the laboratory.

In the laboratory, double-auction markets have very strong *convergence* properties and exhibit particularly high *market efficiency*, as measured by the percentage of the total potential surplus captured

---

[26] I am indebted to Malcolm Coate, Andrew Kleit, and Rene Bustamante (1992) for use of their data set.

[27] I am indebted to John Morris, former FTC Assistant to the Director of Antitrust, for suggesting the parallel to me.

by the traders (or alternatively, the absence of dead weight loss). The tendency for contract prices to converge from the side of the market that has the greater theoretical surplus is well documented.[28]

Figure 1 presents the cost and value assignments for a double-auction experiment and the resulting market performance with four buyers and four sellers inexperienced in laboratory markets.[29] Each seller (buyer) is assigned costs (redemption values) for three units of the experimental commodity. For instance, Buyer 1's redemption value (denoted B1 on Figure 1) for the first unit purchased is $5.65. The experimenter guarantees to redeem Buyer 1's first unit for $5.65. Thus, Buyer 1 earns the difference between the redemption value of the unit and the price he pays for it. As indicated in Figure 1, the redemption values for Buyer 1's second unit is $4.60, and the third $4.45. Similarly, Buyer 2 is assigned redemption values of $4.95, $4.75, and $4.50 for the first, second, and third units purchased. On the supply-side, units of the commodity are produced to order in this market, so that sellers do not bear the cost of production or inventory for unsold units.[30] Seller 1's cost (denoted by S1 in Figure 1) of producing the first unit is $3.75. Seller one earns the difference between the price at which he sells the unit and his cost. His production cost for the second unit is $4.80, and the third, $4.95. Redemption value and cost assignments did not change with trading period; each seller (buyer) faced the same costs (values) for three units each period. By the fourth round of trading, prices have stabilized at the

---

[28] For example, if the surplus is distributed asymmetrically such that the consumers surplus exceeds producers surplus at the static competitive equilibrium, prices will tend to converge to the competitive equilibrium from above. *See* Smith and Williams (1982).

[29] The market design and data presented in Figure 1 are reported in Ketcham, Smith, and Williams (1984).

[30] *See* Mestleman, Welland, and Welland (1987) and Mestleman and Welland (1988) for analysis of inventory effects in laboratory markets.

competitive level. The competitive exchange quantity of seven units is a Nash equilibrium in this market.[31] Appendix 1 provides sample instructions for a seller in a hand-run double auction market.[32]

Other experiments have also shown that four buyers and four sellers can be sufficient to assure rapid and consistent achievement of the competitive price in double-auction markets. These results are robust with nonstationary demand and supply parameters. In other words, when the market demand and supply schedules change over time, the competitive prediction continues to describe the observed market performance.[33] Laboratory research in markets with nonstationary demand and supply schedules suggests the importance of *not* enforcing price discrimination laws. In a dynamic setting with nonstationary demand and supply schedules, the convergence to a new competitive equilibrium *requires* that different prices be charged to different customers. Thus, enforcement (or threat of enforcement) of price discrimination laws, such as the Robinson-Patman Act, in a dynamic setting likely would perversely encourage anticompetitive outcomes. Charging different prices to different customers in a dynamic market is consistent with competition.

In double-auction *duopoly* markets the outcomes remain competitive.[34] In fact, even with *one* seller, the hypothesis of monopoly pricing often is rejected in the double-auction institution.[35] Figure

---

[31] This is to say that if all but one seller offered (buyer bid for) each profitable unit at the competitive equilibrium price, the remaining participant could not do better than to offer (bid for) each profitable unit at the competitive equilibrium price.

[32] Double auction and other experiments either are hand-run, without the use of a computer network, or computer-run. Using the latter method involves assigning each market participant to a computer terminal, which is networked to the other participant's terminals, at which they can enter decisions and receive market feedback.

[33] *See* Miller, Plott, and Smith (1977); Williams (1979); Smith (1982a); Cox and Oaxaca (1990); Davis and Williams (1990a); and Davis, Harrison, and Williams (1993). Hoffman and Plott (1981) also supports this finding when speculators or "middlemen" are present.

[34] Smith and Williams (1989).

[35] *See*, for example, Smith (1981a); Smith and Williams (1981); and Smith and Williams (1989).

2 shows data from a single seller, five buyer double-auction market.[36] The buyers in this market session signal one another by bidding low, strategically *withholding demand* so as to mitigate the power of the monopolist, who does not know the true demand curve. Withholding demand occurs when at least one buyer refuses to purchase units of the laboratory commodity, even when his marginal valuation for a unit exceeds the posted price. The seller(s) relies on the observed buyer behavior to estimate demand. Thus, if buyers under-reveal their true willingness-to-pay then the demand curve is altered in effect. The buyers withhold demand with the intention of influencing the future pricing decisions of the seller(s). The laboratory data on withholding show that the true competitive equilibrium is often preserved. In fact, the misrepresentations of the buyers encourages the competitive outcome. In the market presented in Figure 2, the buyers effectively exert downward pressure on price until the competitive outcome is achieved. Some double-auction monopolists are able to sustain prices above the competitive equilibrium; however, they usually are unable to sustain prices and profits at the level predicted by traditional monopoly theory. These results point to the inadequacies of monopoly theory that abstract from the institution and imperfect information by the participants.

The data from double-auction experiments have profound implications for traditional competitive price theory. The laboratory results show that the competitive equilibrium is attainable with less stringent informational assumptions than thought necessary. The data indicate that each double-auction trader needs only know his own valuations; extensive knowledge of other traders' demand or cost valuations is not necessary to generate a stable competitive outcome. Moreover, the results show that the market need not involve a "large" number of buyers and sellers to achieve competitive results.[37] Trading

---

[36] The market design and data presented in Figure 2 are from Smith and Williams (1989).

[37] This is evident even in the early double-auction experiments (*see*, for instance Smith (1962, 1964). Even though the "large numbers" condition remains in many textbook explanations of competition (*see*, for example, Carlton and Perloff (1989) p. 67), theorists also recognize that the number of buyers and sellers required to achieve competitive outcomes in an industry is analytically unimportant. *See*, for

(continued...)

14

experience is also not imperative to achieve competitive market performance, although experience may speed convergence. Moreover, the results do not require the standard assumption that agents must be "price takers" for the competitive equilibrium to be attained. In the double-auction institution, every trader is a price *maker*.[38] Thus, in the double-auction institution, the competitive prediction is more robust than theory indicates.

Thus, the results from double-auction experiments suggest that there should be limited, if any, antitrust concern in markets with institutional features that resemble those of the double-auction.[39] The strength of competitive tendencies in the double-auction institution arise from the ability of both sides of the market, buyers and sellers, to have a voice in the market. Buyers make bids to buy and sellers make offers to sell, both can accept or reject contracts. To the extent that an antitrust market exhibits such institutional features, experimental evidence offers little support for anticompetitive concerns.

2. The Posted-Offer Institution

Fred Williams (1973) was the first to examine experimentally the posted-offer institution, in which each seller sets production capacity (maximum output) and posts a "take-it-or-leave-it" unit price.[40] Sellers produce to order, so that no inventories are carried from one period to the next, and

---

[37](...continued)
instance, McGee (1971) or Fama and Laffer (1972). Demsetz (1973, p. 26) points out that "there has been an irresistible inclination among economists to identify real world monopoly power with the structure postulate of the monopoly model -- the one-firm industry. It is but a short step from this to the conviction that market concentration is an index of monopoly power."

[38] Each trader can actively participate in the pricing process: buyers make bids and sellers make offers. *See* Smith (1962, 1964, 1976a, and 1982a); Ketcham, Smith, and Williams (1984); and Plott and Smith (1978).

[39] Further evidence, presented below, enhances this conclusion.

[40] This analysis of the posted-offer institution was actually an attempt to compare the single unit per agent endowment feature of the Smith (1962 and 1964) double-auction experiments to a double-auction in which traders are permitted to buy or sell more than one unit per trading period. However, when altering the number of units per trader, Williams also unintentionally modified several of the trading
(continued...)

no production costs are incurred for unordered units. Each seller chooses his price before knowing his rivals' prices. Buyers are selected in random order each period and take turns completing their purchases. A trading period consists of a round of posting prices followed by shopping. When the lowest price producer exhausts his quantity offered for the period, buyers move on to the next lowest price producer, and so on. All buyers may not be satisfied.

The posted-offer institution parallels several features of naturally-occurring retail markets. Sellers in retail markets set production capacities and post prices that cannot be easily changed for some interval. For instance, catalog marketers are unlikely to change their prices until the next issue. Airlines post special rates that are good for travel within certain dates. Stock-outs (hitting capacity constraints within a trading period) are also observed in both retail and posted-offer markets. Sometimes retailers post prices with disclaimers such as "while supplies last" or "subject to available seating." In the laboratory posted-offer institution sellers generally do not incur the cost of units that are not sold. Thus, subject to capacity constraints, production meets demand.

Plott and Smith (1978) and Ketcham, Smith, and Williams (1984) demonstrate that changing the institution from a double-auction to a posted-offer auction can affect outcomes. Prices tend to be higher on average over time in the posted-offer institution than in the double-auction institution. However, and more importantly from an antitrust perspective, prices in both market institutions converge to the competitive price. The reason that posted-offer prices tend to be higher on average than double-auction prices is that in posted-offer markets prices usually converge from above and take longer to adjust to the

---

[40](...continued)
rules. These modifications change the institution from a double-auction to what is commonly known today as a posted-offer auction. Williams reports behavior that is somewhat different than the behavior observed in the Smith single unit per trader double-auctions. Notice that the hypothesis Williams is testing is compound, contaminating the pure effect of moving from a single to a multiple unit assignment of costs and values in the same institution. Plott and Smith (1978) recognize this problem. They also classify and then test the difference between the double-auction and posted-offer institutions.

competitive level.[41] Market efficiency is higher in double-auction markets than in comparable posted-offer markets.[42]

When sellers produce in advance, rather than to demand, and there is no carry over of inventory from one period to the next, the mean price across the two institutions no longer differs significantly. However, the double-auction remains more efficient, because more unsold units are produced in the posted-offer institution. Thus, the production characteristics of an institution may have an impact on market performance.[43]

In contrast to double-auction settings, buyers do not possess the ability to signal in posted-offer markets. While buyers can reject posted offers, these decisions are private (between buyer and seller), eliminating a means to signal to other buyers. Sellers, on the other hand, maintain the ability to signal to other sellers via pricing decisions, which are posted for all market participants to see. Figure 3 presents data from a posted-offer market with experienced sellers.[44] The underlying market structure

---

[41] Davis and Williams (1986) find that, unlike in double-auction markets, posted-offer contract prices converge to competitive equilibrium from above, irrespective of the asymmetry between producers' and consumers' surplus. The institutional effect also interacts with other design parameters. For instance, Ketcham, Smith, and Williams (1984) report that posted-offer markets in which the competitive equilibrium is not Nash, and prices still converge towards the competitive equilibrium with four buyers and four sellers. In posted-offer markets with only two of three sellers active at the competitive equilibrium, the observed prices lie closer to the Nash equilibrium than to the competitive or the limit price equilibrium. But in each case the Nash equilibrium was computed *assuming* that buyers fully reveal demand (otherwise it would be difficult to calculate).

[42] This comparison of institutions is conducted holding all else equal. Thus, while the posted-offer markets exhibit lower levels of market efficiency than double-auction markets, in practice there remains the issue of institution efficiency. For example, consider grocery shopping under the two alternative institutions. The transactions costs of negotiating the price of each of many items under the double-auction trading rules could be substantial and avoided by trading according to posted-offer rules. In general, the gain from avoiding such transactions costs in retail settings by employing a posted-offer institution likely will dominate the loss in market efficiency from not adopting the double-auction trading rules.

[43] Mestelman, Welland and Welland (1987) and Mestelman and Welland (1988).

[44] The sellers have participated previously in posted-offer laboratory markets.

is the same as that of the double-auction experiment presented in Figure 1.[45] However, for the posted-offer trial displayed in Figure 3, attempts are made to create conditions under which tacit collusion would have a good chance of being observed, by recruiting the sellers on the basis of their prior propensity to collude tacitly.[46] Although some signaling efforts (attempts to encourage supracompetitive pricing) arise in the early periods, they are eventually aborted. The trial can hardly be classified as a case of successful collusion. Prices stabilize at the competitive level. Ketcham, Smith, and Williams attribute the slight increase in price during the later periods to "end effect."[47]

Recall that in the double-auction institution, the monopoly model has little predictive power. The monopoly prediction does a better job of describing behavior in posted-offer markets with single sellers. Yet, while the prices lie above the competitive equilibrium in most of the posted-offer markets studied, the index of monopoly effectiveness (the percentage of theoretical monopoly profits actually captured by the single seller) is seldom 100 percent. For instance, across the posted-offer monopoly sessions reported in Isaac, Ramey, and Williams (1983), the average index of monopoly effectiveness is 35 percent.[48] The Isaac, Ramey, and Williams study uses *human* buyers. Brown-Kruse (1986) shows that when demand is fully revealed (generally the case when human buyers are replaced by *simulated buyers*) sellers

---

[45] The demand and cost parameters across the two experiments differ by a constant, $0.55, but the underlying structure is the same.

[46] *See* Ketcham, Smith, and Williams.

[47] Because subjects were experienced, they probably had a reasonable idea that the experiment would end around period 25. Generally, participants are not informed of the number of periods to be conducted in a given market session. Despite the end effect concerns, the buyers reject several offers, swiftly reacting to the sellers' attempt to raise price in the final periods of trading. This disciplining by the buyers was successful in the early trading periods of this market, and likely would have succeeded again if the market continued for longer. The continued efficacy of such attempts to discipline the sellers could be tested directly by increasing the number of periods.

[48] The per-period measures range from -222% to 100%.

extract more rents from posted-offer markets. This suggests that when sellers lack complete information on demand, human buyers can strategically influence the market outcome.[49]

B. Oligopoly

1. Institutions and Information

Theory presents several alternative models of oligopoly. The laboratory permits the examination of different institutions suggested by the theories, as well as the impact of various information conditions upon market performance. Many oligopoly experiments use either double-auction or posted-offer institutions, but other institutions such as Cournot[50] and Bertrand[51] are also studied. In both Cournot and Bertrand settings, the market demand curve is provided to all sellers. In Cournot markets, sellers set quantities; in Bertrand markets, they set price.

As first shown by Carlson (1967) for large markets (more than 20 sellers), and later by Wellford (1989) for oligopolies (five firms), quantity-setting markets that are theoretically unstable in the cobweb or Cournot sense exhibit strong convergence properties in laboratory markets. Subjects behave "as if" the markets are stable. The hypothesis that subjects form expectations consistent with the cobweb model, *i.e.*, that price next period will be the same as price in the current period, is not supported by laboratory

---

[49] Monopoly theory also encounters difficulties in a *posted-bid* institution. Smith (1982) shows that in markets with *one* seller who can accept or reject bids, and five buyers who post bids (a posted-*bid* as opposed to a posted-*offer* institution), monopoly power is not exercised. This results because the buyers successfully signal other buyers via their bids to withhold their true willingness-to-pay. Thus, through misrepresenting their willingness-to-pay, the buyers neutralize the seller's monopoly power, because the seller does not know the true demand curve. Market price and production converge to the competitive prediction in this institution and environment.

[50] *See*, for instance, Fouraker and Siegel, *ibid*; Binger, Hoffman, Libecap, and Schachat (1990); and Wellford (1990).

[51] *See*, for example, Friedman (1967) and Friedman and Hoggatt (1980); and Hoggatt, Friedman, and Gill (1967).

tests. Further, rational expectations also fails to predict well. Of the traditional models considered, adaptive and extrapolative expectations best describe the data.[52] However, the structure, not just the parameterization, of expectations seems to be adaptive. Market participants alter their expectation process when they realize that their myopic responses lead to relatively unfavorable outcomes.[53]

Information plays an important role in laboratory markets. Most oligopoly theories require *complete* and *common information* on preferences to achieve noncooperative equilibria.[54] This raises issues for applied work in antitrust and other areas, as it is difficult to believe that each market participant in the naturally-occurring economy actually knows the utility values for all other participants. In the laboratory competitive and noncooperative equilibrium outcomes are more likely to arise behaviorally however, under the conditions of *private information* than under complete information.[55] If *sellers* actually had complete information, they often would prefer to achieve a different equilibrium.[56]

---

[52] It is interesting to note that macro theorists are reverting from rational to adaptive expectations. *See*, for instance, Thomas Sargent's address in honor of Milton Friedman's eightieth birthday at the 1992 Western Economic Association meetings.

[53] Wellford, *ibid*. Schmalensee (1976) finds in a stark (nonmarket) setting that the speed of response in the adaptive structure retards during turning points. *See* Grether (1980 and 1992) and Camerer (1987) for tests of Bayes rule.

[54] Complete information holds when each market agent knows the preferences of all the other agents. Common information holds when all of the agents have information, and they know that all of the other agents possess this information and so forth.

[55] Complete information in the laboratory generally refers to information on the payout functions and previous decisions of other market participants. Under conditions of private information in the laboratory, market participants know only how their own decisions affect their payout, and can observe the market outcomes (*i.e.*, the market price and market production level). For other discussions on the effect of complete information in laboratory markets, *see* Smith (1989) and (1990), and McCabe, Rassenti, and Smith (1989). Holt (1985) conducts a quantity-choice duopoly game under complete information, and notes that the subjects want to earn more than the other firm, yet show no tendency to maximize the difference between their earnings. He conjectures that there "...probably would have been less variability in the data if the subjects in these experiments had not been given the complete information necessary to compute the other seller's profits," (p. 323).

[56] In general, symmetric Cournot duopolists can earn more by choosing the joint profit maximization equilibrium rather than playing the noncooperative (Cournot) strategy.

Fouraker and Siegel (1963) document the effect of complete versus private information in their study of Cournot and Bertrand duopolies and triopolies. Tables 1 and 2 summarize Fouraker and Siegel's results, which have been confirmed in many other environments and institutions. The tables provide the percentage of sessions in which the market quantity (price) in a Cournot (Bertrand) market converges to (or near) a particular equilibrium concept after a specified number of periods.[57] Sellers in complete information treatments know the profit functions of their rivals. In particular, sellers know how each rival's quantity decision affects the rival's profit. In the private information treatments, each seller knows only his own profit function. Referring to Table 1, duopolies in the reported quantity choice markets under private information show no support for the shared monopoly outcome (*i.e.*, the joint maximum), and the strongest support (87.5%) for the Cournot equilibrium.[58] By contrast, the joint maximum equilibrium concept received support in 31.25% of the Cournot markets conducted under conditions of complete information. While the Cournot prediction continues to describe behavior in 46.87% of the markets, it has diminished predictive power relative to the otherwise equivalent private information treatments. The ability of the noncooperative equilibria (*i.e.*, Cournot and Bertrand) to predict also improves under conditions of private information for the both Cournot triopoly and Bertrand duopoly markets. Table 2 suggests that the incentives in the Bertrand markets are sufficient to overcome the information effect as the number of sellers increases, so that the Bertrand equilibrium predicts well under both information treatments.

The ability of markets to economize information (*i.e.*, without intending to, market agents achieve efficient outcomes) was recognized by Adam Smith (1776) in his discussion of the invisible hand and

---

[57] Fouraker and Siegel report data for period 21 in the Cournot markets, and period 14 in the Bertrand markets. A period is one round during which sellers set quantity (price) in each Cournot (Bertrand) market session.

[58] This is not to say that the Cournot equilibrium was observed in 87.5% of the markets during period 21, rather that the observations lie *closer* to the Cournot prediction than to the alternative equilibria of interest.

described in more detail by Hayek (1945). However, until the advent of laboratory methods, it was difficult to test *directly* whether this hypothesis would hold. At least through the mid-fifties, the economics profession at large did not accept the relevance of the claim.[59] In fact, before he started conducting laboratory experiments, Vernon Smith (1993), who some call the "father" of experimental methods in economics, also doubted its applicability until his experimental subjects convinced him otherwise.

> In many experimental markets, poorly informed, error-prone, and uncomprehending human agents interact through the trading rules to produce social algorithms which demonstrably approximate the wealth maximizing outcomes traditionally thought to require complete information and cognitively rational actors.

While the outcomes of Smith's early experiments supported the notion that markets economize information,[60] Smith (1982a) provides a more stringent test of the Hayek Hypothesis, which he specifies as (p. 167):

> Strict privacy together with the trading rules of a market institution are sufficient to produce competitive market outcomes at or near 100% efficiency.

Using the double auction institution, three treatments are considered: (1) stationary, (2) cyclical, and (3) irregular shifts in demand and supply. Figure 4 presents the data from one laboratory session conducted under the most rigorous design reported. The data are representative of other sessions conducted under the same design. In this market, after the first week of trading (five periods), the demand and supply schedules shift from D_1 and S_1 to D_2 and S_2. The four sellers have identical unit costs of $5.70, with an 11 unit aggregate production capacity during the first week and a 16 unit one in the second. The four buyers have the same unit value of $6.80, with the aggregate capacity to demand no more than 16 units

---

[59] As Smith (1993) notes, the Chicago and Austrian schools of thought were the exceptions. *See also* Kitch (1983) for a remembrance of the days at Chicago prior to the general professional acceptance of these ideas.

[60] *See* Smith (1962 and 1964).

22

during the first week, and no more than 11 units the second.[61] The competitive equilibrium during the first (second) week occurs at the price of $6.80 ($5.70) with an output of 11 (11) units. This market design provides a rigorous "stress test" of the Hayek Hypothesis. The competitive equilibrium is not the unique price and production mix which satisfies 100% market efficiency. Complete efficiency occurs when 11 units are sold at *any* price ranging from $5.70 to $6.80. This provides a stringent test of the ability of price to converge to the competitive equilibrium in this design, because at the competitive equilibrium during week one (week two) all of the $12.10 per period exchange surplus accrues to the sellers (buyers). Thus, at the competitive equilibrium during the first week (second week), buyers (sellers) receive only a 10¢ trading commission per unit exchanged. The extreme asymmetry of the exchange surplus between buyers and sellers creates tremendous incentives for the market agents that are cut out of the exchange surplus at the competitive equilibrium to exert more resistance in the bargaining process. Such resistance could curtail, if not prevent, convergence to the competitive equilibrium.

The results presented in Figure 4 reveal an slow but steady convergence of price to the competitive solution by periods four and five in week one. It appears as though sellers' expectations of high prices and profits initially retard the rate of convergence after the shift in the demand and cost schedules. However, the new competitive equilibrium is achieved by periods nine and ten. These data provide impressive support for the Hayek Hypothesis in an environment with stationary demand and supply curves in the double-auction institution. Smith (1984b) also finds strong support for the hypothesis in experiments with dynamic environments. Van Boening and Wilcox (1992) have constructed markets with avoidable fixed costs in a double-auction institution. Their markets provide an even greater challenge to the ability of the market to achieve the competitive outcome, and have spawned research

---

[61] Market participants are not informed in advance that market conditions might change. Smith (1982a, p. 172) notes that "from the point of view of the participants this change is rather subtle in that their individual value and cost assignments remain constant." Only the aggregate demand and supply capacities change.

efforts to explore and design institutions that overcome more effectively the lumpiness inherent in such cost functions.[62]

Another interesting informational finding relates to situations of asymmetric information. Camerer, Lowenstein, and Weber (1989) find evidence that supports a popular theory in psychology, that better informed agents often fall victim to the "curse of knowledge." The curse occurs when agents fail to ignore information that they have that others do not, even when it is unnecessary information. For instance, investment bankers, who possess more information than the public about a stock to be offered publicly, must anticipate the demand for the securities by the relatively uninformed public when pricing the shares.[63]

The curse runs contrary to the conventional assumption in agency theory that agents with better information can correctly forecast the decisions of less informed agents.[64] More information may not always be an advantage. This is not to say that no information is necessarily better than some. In fact, the anticompetitive distortions of asymmetric information outcomes can be overcome in markets.[65] Market forces in the double-auction institution decrease the magnitude of the "curse" by about 50%, this decrease is largely due to the more rational traders disproportionate share of actions in the market. Thus, the disciplining forces of the market promote the paradox that individual irrationality can encourage collective rationality.

---

[62] *See*, for instance, Durham, Rassenti, Smith, Van Boening, and Wilcox (1993).

[63] Other examples include fashion, wine, and movies. Industry experts have informed opinions about the value of the product, but if they are subject to the curse of knowledge their prices will tend to biased upward (downward) for high (low) quality items relative to the uninformed general public's willingness to pay, and thus also relative to the profit maximizing level.

[64] *See* Conn, Young, and Bishop (1991) for tests of principal-agent theory.

[65] *See*, for instance, Isaac, Ramey, and Williams (1984).

The curse is otherwise difficult to erode, even with very large incentives and extensive training, learning does not improve much. The curse remains. Camerer *et al.* note that the curse could affect strategic behavior in oligopoly settings, as firms erroneously decide to enter or exit. However, this remains to be tested. The curse has also yet to be analyzed in a systematic fashion in other laboratory institutions. Such study may enhance our knowledge of the breadth of the curse and the ability of markets to overcome it.

2. Market Power

The role of information, the form of institution, and other factors come into play in laboratory studies of market power. *Market power*, classified as a "unilateral competitive effect" by the Horizontal Merger Guidelines (1992, §2.2), is the ability of a firm to maintain price above the competitive level unilaterally and profitably. *Equilibrium Market Power*, a general game-theoretic concept, refers to a noncooperative equilibrium that is consistent with supracompetitive prices.

The laboratory facilitates the analysis of market power, in that it can be built explicitly into the structure of the market. Thus, the behavioral consequence of the existence of market power can be compared directly to markets that are identical except for the lack of market power.

Figure 5 presents a market design in which unilateral market power exists in a noncooperative game.[66] At the competitive equilibrium in this market with five sellers, 16 units are produced at the price of $2.60. In order to encourage the purchase and sale of the marginal units, each market participant receives a 5¢ commission per unit exchanged.[67] Either of the low cost sellers, seller one (S1) or seller two (S2), could unilaterally and profitably increase their price from $2.60 to $2.85. At the competitive equilibrium, the two low-cost sellers would each earn $2.60 per unit for five units of production, less the

---

[66] This design originates in Holt, Langan, and Villamil (1986) and is implemented in several subsequent laboratory studies on market power.

[67] Plott and Smith (1978) find that 5¢ commissions are sufficient to motivate marginal trades.

$11.50 cost of producing the five units, plus $.25 in commissions, for earnings of $1.75.[68] However, assuming that the other sellers behave competitively, if either seller one or seller two withholds its two zero-profit units from sale, the *effective* supply curve shifts back so that the *effective* competitive equilibrium, where the demand and (effective) supply schedules cross, occurs at the price of $2.85. At this price, the seller who suppresses production by two units would earn $2.40, including commissions. Hence, it is profitable for either seller one or seller two to unilaterally increase price above the fundamental competitive equilibrium. In this example, the other low-cost seller, who withholds no units of production from the market would earn $3.00. Hence in this example, the two low-cost sellers increase their earnings by either $0.65 or $1.25. Any of the high-cost sellers (sellers three, four, and five) could also withhold a unit, and unilaterally and profitably increase price above the competitive level, but not as dramatically as the low-cost sellers. Unilaterally withholding one unit from the market would lead to a price between $2.60 and $2.85, thus a high-cost seller would increase his earnings by no more than 20¢ and could decrease it by less than 5¢.[69]

Table 3 presents a terse summary of several laboratory studies of market power.[70] I briefly discuss the overall findings of the research and some of the issues that they raise.

a). *Supracompetitive Pricing, Efficiency, and the Hayek Hypothesis*

While not consistently observed across all design treatments, supracompetitive pricing does occur in some of the laboratory markets. Probably the most striking result across the studies is that *even when market power is built into the structure of the market, the observed market efficiency remains relatively*

---

[68] As Figure 4 indicates, seller one (or two) incurs production costs of $1.60 for the first unit, $2.35 per unit for the second and third units, and $2.60 per unit for the fourth and fifth units.

[69] Withholding two units would unilaterally make the effective competitive equilibrium occur at the price $2.85, however any high-cost seller doing so would forego earnings altogether.

[70] Several of the studies (*see*, for instance, Holt and Davis (1990)) include a baseline treatment which are similar to the other treatments as possible except that no market power exists. These baseline market trials are not included in Table 3.

high. Thus, the deadweight loss associated with the presence of theoretical market power seems to be small in laboratory markets.

What do the results of supracompetitive pricing and high market efficiency imply when evaluated in the context of the Hayek Hypothesis? One, interpretation of the Hayek Hypothesis, the *price interpretation*, implies that prices should converge to the competitive level. Another interpretation, the *efficiency interpretation*, suggests that the surplus captured should approach 100%. Davis and Williams (1991) find that when sellers recognize they possess market power, the price interpretation is often violated in double-auction and posted-offer markets. However, the efficiency interpretation of the hypothesis cannot be rejected, even when the price interpretation fails to hold. Across the studies reported in Table 3, the average market efficiencies consistently exceed 90%.[71]

Several of the studies note that sellers with theoretical market power rarely withhold units in the manner that static market power theory predicts. For instance, Davis and Williams (1991, p. 270) report that across their eight posted-offer markets the two low-cost sellers

> offered less than nine of the ten units collectively available to them in only eight out of one hundred and forty six periods. Five of these instances occurred in the first two periods of trading in four different experiments, while the remaining three instances were isolated instances in three different experiments.

The authors also report that one of four of their double-auction trials exhibits evidence of strategic withholding by sellers one and two. Yet, these low-cost sellers fail to achieve prices that are significantly higher than those in the other double-auction trials.

These unexpected results could be due to the fact that sellers in the laboratory markets do not recognize that they have potential market power. Only in a few cases does experience with the institution seem to increase the sellers' awareness of their potential market influence to the point that they attempt

---

[71] A few studies do not report efficiencies.

to exercise their power.[72]   The general absence of withholding in these markets suggests that the observed supracompetitive pricing is due to tacit collusion rather than the exercise of market power. When market power exists, the likelihood of tacit collusion increases; yet, the achievement of perfect collusion is infrequently observed.[73]

It is not clear that the observed supracompetitive pricing is due to the presence of theoretical market power in the markets considered. Smith (1965) reports similar results (supracompetitive prices with high market efficiencies) in double-auction markets *without* market power but otherwise comparable to the Holt, Langan, and Villamil (1986) market design. The relevant common design feature appears to be the small excess supply at the competitive equilibrium (one unit in Holt, Langan, and Villamil, two units in Smith). This issue can be addressed in the laboratory with minor design alterations.

b). *Institution Matters*

When controlling for market power, larger deviations from the competitive equilibrium are observed in posted-offer markets than in double-auction markets.[74]   The differential impact is most obvious when the *buyers*, rather than the sellers, have market power. When buyers have market power

---

[72] Holt, Langan, and Villamil (1986) find one experienced seller who figures out the advantages of withholding. However, other studies (*e.g.*, *see* Davis and Williams (1991)) find no evidence of increased incidence of withholding of production by experienced participants. Another way to increase the sellers' familiarity with their potential market power would involve establishing the condition of complete information, so that each seller knows the cost and payoff functions of his rivals. It could also be important to require the sellers to "earn the right" to be in a position of potential power. Hoffman and Spitzer (1982) find that in laboratory tests of bargaining that if the preferential property rights are randomly assigned rather than "earned" (through a trivial game) that participants are less likely to fully exercise those rights. This would make it clear to all sellers and buyers (when human buyers are used) that there exist fundamental differences in cost structures across sellers. Barring these two design changes, complete information and "earned" assignment of property rights, it is unlikely that the opportunities to the sellers could be made clearer.

[73] *See*, for instance, Davis, Holt, and Villamil (1990).

[74] *See*, for instance, Holt (1989) and Davis and Williams (1991).

in double-auction markets, they are able to elicit subcompetitive prices,[75] however in posted-offer markets they are unable to overcome the institutional asymmetry (*i.e.*, that buyers cannot post bids, but sellers can post offers - - so that buyers have a more indirect influence on price) and prices converge to the competitive equilibrium.

Friedman and Ostroy (1991) argue that in most recent laboratory studies of market power, market agents have the opportunity to trade only a few units of an indivisible commodity. This indivisibility significantly reduces the profitable opportunities to raise price by withholding units. As the authors point out, in some markets the only way a trader can influence price is by exiting from the market and therefore giving up all profit for the trading period. When divisibility of sales is incorporated, it affects the ability of sellers to exercise market power in the double-auction institution. Most notably, when divisibility is allowed, supracompetitive pricing is not observed. Friedman and Ostroy describe the behavior of the market participants (p. 3),

> Through their misrepresentations, the subjects spontaneously imposed a perfectly competitive environment on each other...[the institution with divisibility] encourages individuals with potential monopoly power to exercise that power in such a way that it is neutralized.

Another institutional feature that affects the exercise of market power involves whether the message space of the buyers is limited to include only their true reservation values, as is often the case when buyers are simulated rather than human. As found in other environments under the posted-offer institution, prices are significantly lower when human buyers are present than when buyers are simulated to behave as the theory predicts.[76] Davis and Williams (1991) find that when human buyers are present and sellers have market power, price converges to the competitive equilibrium in posted-offer markets.

---

[75] This is found in one of two buyer-power market trials (not summarized in Table 3) from the Holt, Langan, and Villamil (1986) study. This trial, which has a symmetric distribution of exchange surplus between buyers and sellers, establishes that contracts occurring at prices below the competitive equilibrium are not due solely to the asymmetric distribution of exchange surplus (*see supra* note 24).

[76] *See* Brown-Kruse (1986 and 1991).

While the data from experiments reveal that institutions matter, the data also suggest that a feature of the environment, the nature of aggregate production capacity at the competitive equilibrium, might determine whether market power will in fact be exercised or whether tacit collusion is more effectively achieved. When aggregate production capacity of the market is constrained at the competitive equilibrium, the likelihood of supracompetitive pricing might be different than when this aggregate capacity is nonbinding. The column in Table 3 marked "excess capacity at CE" indicates whether the production capacity is nonbinding. This issue is discussed in greater detail in the next section, as it also arises in research on the effect of communication upon collusion.

3. Tacit and Explicit Conspiracies in Restraint of Trade

Many laboratory studies of oligopoly focus on tacit or explicit conspiracy.[77] The laboratory provides a useful mechanism for studying conspiracies. By controlling directly the communication of market participants (*e.g.*, whether or what kind of communication is allowed), the impact of explicit versus tacit conspiracy can be compared to theoretical predictions. Collusion is studied in several laboratory institutions, including the Cournot, double-auction, and posted-offer auction.[78]

a). *Opportunities for Tacit Collusion*

Permitting communication only through the choice variables specified by the theory and institution allows tests of the ability of sellers to collude tacitly. In other words, sellers have no means of communicating directly with each other except through their market decisions.

---

[77] R. M. Isaac (1990) provides a useful overview.

[78] *See* Isaac and Walker (1985) and Gerety (1987) for worthwhile laboratory studies of collusion in sealed-bid and sealed-offer auctions. Examples of these institutions in field markets include the application of sealed-bid auctions to assign off-shore oil leases, and sealed-offer auctions to select procurement contractors.

In Cournot industries with *more than two sellers*, prices tend to lie between the static Cournot and competitive predictions, the joint profit maximum (*i.e.*, the monopoly outcome) is not achieved.[79] Theoretically, the Cournot solution approaches the competitive level as the number of sellers increases. Behaviorally, the fewer the number of sellers, the higher the observed variance in prices in laboratory quantity-setting markets.[80]

In laboratory Cournot *duopolies*, the behavioral results are less clear. Binger, Hoffman, Libecap, and Schachat (1990) observe prices converging to the collusive outcome from above the Cournot-Nash equilibrium under conditions of complete information, while Morrison and Kamarei (1990) find successful collusion in only one of their eight laboratory duopolies conducted under conditions of incomplete information. Under complete information in quantity-choice duopoly games, the Cournot-Nash equilibrium predicts better than the consistent conjectures and the collusive equilibria.[81]

Similar mixed results arise in price-choice institutions with two sellers. Dolbear, Lave, and Bowman (1966) mention more variability in outcomes with duopolies than with triopolies in price-setting markets. Davis, Holt, and Villamil (1990) also find that some duopolies exhibit rivalistic behavior in posted-offer markets. Benson and Faminow (1988) show that subject experience with the institution increases the incidence of tacit collusion in posted-offer duopolies, but they too observe experienced participants who compete fiercely. So, while tacit collusion between two sellers appears to be easier to coordinate than when there are more sellers in laboratory markets, head-on competition is also observed in duopolies.

---

[79] This is found in many studies. *See*, for instance, Fouraker and Siegel, *ibid*; Binger, Hoffman, Libecap, and Schachat (1990); and Morrison and Kamarei (1990).

[80] *See*, for instance, Fouraker and Siegel (1963) and Wellford (1990).

[81] *See* Holt (1985). At the consistent conjectures equilibrium, each firm knows the other's output choice and, given the conjectured reaction of the other firm, any deviation from their own output level would be unprofitable.

Posner (1976) points out that the concentration level at which concerns of collusive pricing arise depends on the economist. For instance, Scherer (1970 p. 185) would be concerned when the four largest firms hold a forty percent industry share. Bork (1978 pp. 221-222), on the other hand, argues:

> we are in the area of uncertainty when we ask whether mergers that would concentrate a market to only two firms of roughly equal size should be prohibited. My guess is that they should not and, therefore, that mergers up to 60 or 70 percent of the market should be permitted - a figure, curiously enough, that resembles the old Sherman Act..."

Bork also suggests that horizontal mergers that would create no fewer than three significant firms should be considered presumptively lawful. In general, applying these alternative rules of thumb for identifying presumptively collusive markets, the Bork rule outperforms the Scherer rule in laboratory markets.

Over time, average prices in laboratory posted-offer oligopolies are higher than in otherwise identical double-auctions. With more than two sellers however, prices in both the double-auction and posted-offer institutions eventually converge to competitive levels. Alger (1986, 1987) presents some evidence that longer experiments, which allow participants more time to coordinate a collusive strategy, can lead to more anticompetitive outcomes in posted-offer markets. At present it is not clear how to interpret his results in relation to other studies, as he made numerous design changes.[82]

As discussed in the previous subsection, the structural existence of market power in double-auction and posted-offer institutions sometimes leads to its exercise.[83] More often, it appears to increase the likelihood of tacit collusion. However, even when supracompetitive pricing occurs in the laboratory

---

[82] Some of the changes include the number of sellers, the information available to sellers (*e.g.* quantity sold by rivals), simulated buyer behavior, the number of periods, the length of periods, the instructions, and the cost and demand configurations (*e.g.* a Walrasian excess supply at the competitive equilibrium). Taking one of the changes for instance, as shown by Brown-Kruse (1986 and 1991), altering the buyer rationing process is not a trivial modification. Thus, one cannot attribute the result of making numerous changes simultaneously to any individual change.

[83] *See* Davis and Williams (1990b, 1991); Holt, Langan, and Villamil (1986); Davis, Holt, and Villamil (1990); and Holt (1989).

markets studied, the efficiency loss is generally small.[84] The posted-offer markets adjust more slowly than their double-auction counterparts to capture the gains from exchange. However, Smith (1982c) and Davis and Williams (1990b) find that the posted-offer institution mitigates market power and the ability to tacitly collude when the power is on the nonposting (*i.e.*, the buyers') side. For example, in *posted-bid* markets, in which buyers post bids and sellers accept or reject them, seller market power and tacit collusion is ineffective. Thus, the absence of a voice (*i.e.*, the ability to post either a bid or an offer) in the market appears to explain many of the behavioral differences observed in posted-offer and double-auction monopolies and oligopolies. Laboratory results suggest that the effect of the institution can dominate the effect of market structure, and thus, influence the likelihood of successful tacit collusion.

b) *Opportunities for Explicit Collusion*

Several laboratory studies research the impact of allowing open communication among sellers regarding price and other matters. Explicit communication among sellers about price, the "smoking gun" of antitrust, constitutes a *per se* violation of the Sherman Act in naturally-occurring markets.[85] The experiments with explicit opportunities to collude permit situations that would blatantly violate the antitrust laws in field markets. Thus, the laboratory markets provide benchmarks of behavior in a setting without the threat of antitrust enforcement.[86] Different types of permissible communication, such as communications akin to trade press announcements, can also be considered in laboratory markets.

---

[84] *See* Table 3.

[85] *See*, for instance, *U.S. v. Socony-Vacuum Oil Co. et al.*, 310 U.S. 150 (1940), which remains the precedent of *per se* illegality of explicit horizontal price fixing.

[86] The threat of antitrust enforcement can be incorporated in laboratory tests, although it is not commonly implemented. *See* Gerety (1987).

When communication among sellers is permitted between trading periods in laboratory markets, participants quickly decide that price is an interesting topic to discuss.[87] In laboratory markets with open communication, buyers generally are (1) not informed of the sellers' deliberations, and (2) are physically isolated from the sellers. For example, Isaac, Ramey, and Williams (1984) geographically separate the buyer and sellers. The sellers, located in Arizona, transact with the buyers, who are situated in Indiana, via a computer network.

Even when open communication is permitted in double-auction markets in the laboratory with at least two sellers, prices still converge to the competitive equilibrium. By contrast, in posted-offer markets with at least two sellers, prices tend toward the higher Cournot-Nash equilibrium.[88] Binger *et al.* find that communication facilitates collusion in laboratory Cournot markets, in which sellers set quantity. When communication is permitted in these Cournot experiments, markets with two or five sellers are statistically indistinguishable from the monopoly outcome, *i.e.*, the joint profit maximum is maintained throughout. Brown-Kruse, Cronshaw, and Schenk (1993) show that communication can lead to collusive outcomes in otherwise competitive spatial markets.

Holt and Davis (1990) observe an absence of stable collusive outcomes in posted-offer markets under communications (nonbinding price announcements) of the type traditionally considered in the grey area of antitrust law. This result holds even when market power exists. In other words, in the Holt and Davis experiments, when (1) sellers are provided an opportunity to increase prices unilaterally and

---

[87] Often the participants are prohibited from revealing their individual unit costs and from making side-payments. *See*, for instance, Isaac, Ramey, and Williams (1984).

[88] Note that while prices may be higher in posted-offer duopolies when communication is permitted, the prices do not reach the perfectly collusive (monopoly) level. *See* Isaac, Ramey, and Williams (1984), Isaac and Plott (1981), and Smith (1981a).

profitably by strategically withholding quantity and (2) nonbinding price announcements are made, the sellers do *not* exercise market power.[89]

Davis and Holt (1991) present four experiments showing that market power in posted-offer markets of three and five sellers leads to supracompetitive pricing. This result conflicts with the competitive results Holt and Davis (1990) find in similar markets of three sellers with nonbinding price communication (which would presumably only enhance the erosion of competition). The authors do not compare their 1990 and 1991 papers on market power, and thus they fail to identify the significant design change that seems to be driving the outcomes. The change has to do with the nature of aggregate production capacity. In the 1990 design, aggregate production capacity exceeds the competitive equilibrium level (as in Figure 5); while in the 1991 study, it is constrained at the competitive solution. Thus, it appears that the aggregate capacity constraint promotes the exercise of market power, when it exists. Further research is necessary to complete the analysis of the effect of aggregate production capacity on unilateral market power, with and without nonbinding communication.

In markets not explicitly designed to investigate unilateral market power, Isaac and Reynolds (1990) find that the nature of aggregate capacity at the competitive equilibrium has a significant impact on market performance in posted-offer markets, even more so than a pure numbers effect of moving from four to two sellers. High excess aggregate capacity at the competitive equilibrium encourages more competitive behavior than the low excess aggregate capacity market designs. This supports the examples from the naturally-occurring economy presented in Scherer (1980, pages 209-212),[90] and contests the

---

[89] Before each period, one seller (selected in an announced sequence) is permitted to communicate via a computer network by completing the statement "____ is an appropriate price for the market this period." Other sellers can respond 'A' if they agree, and 'L' ('H') if they think it should be lower (higher). The announcements and responses are displayed to each seller every period.

[90] *See also* the experiments in Sherman (1971); and Brown-Kruse *et al.* (1993), which also shows that when sellers have capacity constraints, market behavior is best described by the Bertrand-Edgeworth "cycling" model. However, while the Bertrand-Edgeworth model predicts better than the mixed-strategy

(continued...)

Davidson and Deneckere (1990) model of excess capacity as a device (a credible threat to punish defectors) to facilitate collusion.[91]

C. Mergers

Wellford (1990) examines horizontal mergers in laboratory Cournot markets. The study considers the ability of the critical levels of concentration demarcated in the *Horizontal Merger Guidelines* (1992) to screen for anticompetitive mergers in controlled markets.[92] Production efficiencies resulting from merger and methods of measuring concentration are considered in the study.

Table 4 presents the basic experimental design. The Cournot markets studied have either five symmetric firms (each with 20% of industry capital -- see column I) or eleven firms (three large, three medium, and five small firms, each with 15%, 10%, and 5% of industry capital, respectively -- see column II) before the merger. The initial market supply and demand conditions are identical for both of the industry structures. In the five-firm industries described in column I, merger creates a new entity with 40% of the industry's capital and increases the Herfindahl-Hirshman Index (HHI) of market concentration from 2000 to 2800. Based on the HHI levels, the Guidelines classify these industries as "highly concentrated" and mergers that "potentially raise significant competitive concern" (§1.51(c)). In the eleven-firm industries characterized in column II, merger occurs between two small firms, increasing the HHI from 1100 to 1150. This corresponds to a merger that the Guidelines state would be unlikely to have adverse competitive consequences and ordinarily require no further analysis" (§1.51(b)).

---

[90](...continued)
Nash equilibrium, the joint monopoly equilibrium, and the competitive equilibrium, each has some predictive power. None of the models is entirely consistent with the laboratory data.

[91] Moreover, the data from the field markets upon which the Isaac and Reynolds (1990) design is based, (*see* Isaac, Oaxaca, and Reynolds (1988)) are consistent with their laboratory results.

[92] The critical levels of concentration did not change in the revision of the 1984 Guidelines.

The performance of the laboratory markets with eleven firms is indeed competitive. Yet, some competitive improvement is apparent when the merged firm enjoys economies of scale.

In light of the laboratory findings relating to complete versus private information conditions, the experiments are conducted under conditions of private information.[93] As in other laboratory investigations of Cournot markets, each seller chooses the quantity to produce and knows the true market demand curve. The experimental design prohibits entry into the laboratory industries.

Figure 6 presents the series of average prices by period from five Cournot laboratory markets with five symmetric firms premerger and four postmerger. No efficiency gains result due to merger in this experimental treatment. All market participants have experience in similar Cournot markets (without merger), so that they are familiar with choosing production quantities and calculating their profits. Figure 7 provides the average price by period from markets that have the same underlying conditions as those shown in Figure 6, except that the merged firm in each of five market sessions enjoys economies of scale in production.

As Fouraker and Siegel found in their study of Cournot private information triopolies,[94] the data in both Figures 6 and 7 tend to lie between the static competitive and Cournot predictions.[95] No tacitly collusive outcomes are observed in *any* individual market session. The market quickly disciplines sellers who try to cut output. Those who reduce production in one period generally increase it in the next.

When the merged firm experiences no economies from merging, the mean postmerger price across all market sessions in this treatment is not significantly greater than the premerger price. The data suggests that the critical HHI levels established by the Guidelines may be overly strict, especially

---

[93] *See* §III B(1), *supra*.

[94] *See* §III B(1), *supra*.

[95] It should be noted that these markets structurally differ from the Cournot markets reported in the previous section. Symmetric firm size is not maintained in these merger experiments, but is standard in the other market studies.

considering that entry is precluded during, and the threat of antitrust enforcement is absent from, the experiments.

Economies of scale due to merger have a statistically significant impact on industry performance in the markets studied; efficiencies make the markets more competitive. Figures 6 and 7 illustrate the downward pressure on mean price by period when the merged firm experiences increasing returns to scale in production. Moreover, a statistically significant increase in mean total surplus and mean consumer surplus is observed. The efficiency result may have implications for mergers in declining industries, as it is generally believed that mergers in such industries exhibit increasing returns to scale cost structures.

The Guidelines state that concentration may be measured by either capacity or sales. Capacity is a control variable set by the experimenter, sales are observable *ex post*. All of the industries studied exhibit significantly higher levels of concentration as measured by sales than when measured based on capacity or on capital. In fact, when measured by sales, the eleven-firm industry HHI increases from 1900 premerger to 2000 postmerger (compared to 1100 to 1150 based on capacity). This measurement discrepancy is enough to move the behaviorally competitive eleven-firm industries into the range of concentration that the Guidelines classify as raising "significant competitive concern." For the mergers studied, relying on the HHI as measured by sales instead of capacity leads to inappropriately increasing the number of cases to be challenged. The laboratory data indicate that basing the HHI on capacity and altering the policy demarcation line would improve measurement of anticompetitive effects.

D. The Illusive Giant: Predation

Isaac and Smith (1985) set out to find predatory pricing under conditions that theory suggests are amenable to predation, noting that (p. 320), "if such behavior is a human trait we ought to be able to observe it in the laboratory." Their design involves two firms: one large firm (firm A) with "deep pockets" and a cost advantage over the other firm, a small firm (firm B). Both firms are given an up front capital endowment to help offset possible future losses. Firm A receives twice the capital endowment of firm B. Figure 8 gives the demand and supply conditions, specifying seller costs and buyer values. The market is structured so that firm A can exclude B and still experience a positive cash flow. The design sufficiently separates the alternative equilibria, including joint monopoly, dominant firm, Edgeworth cycling, predation, and competition.[96] Predation is not observed in this design with or without sunk entry costs to discourage entry. Satisfying the theoretical assumption of complete information on competitors' costs, in addition to sunk entry costs again proves fruitless, as does attempting to induce rivalistic incentives.[97] The dominant firm equilibrium best describes the data from all the treatments.[98] After unsuccessful attempts at creating conditions suitable for observing predation, Isaac and Smith plant a confederate instructed to consistently price at predatory levels, to verify that firm B can indeed be forced to exit in their design. Exit occurs.

Isaac and Smith also study the effect of imposing various antitrust remedies for predation aimed at markets where predation is theoretically likely.[99] In their experimental design, application of a remedy corresponds to a situation of type two regulatory error, as no predation is observed in these

---

[96] This is to say that from each seller's perspective his profit in one equilibrium is sufficiently different than his profit in another (*i.e.* *dominance* in payoffs is satisfied not only over the entire experiment, but also across relevant alternatives at a given point in time). For instance, if each seller's earnings only differ by a cent in one equilibrium versus another, it would be unlikely to observe a clean behavioral separation in market predictions when an experiment is replicated.

[97] Inducing rivalistic incentives raises methodological issues, as it move away from the issue of whether predatory behavior is innately a human trait.

[98] The dominant firm equilibrium (*dfe*) entails firm B following firm A's lead in setting price. For the Isaac and Smith design, both firms set the same price of $2.84 in the *dfe* and firm A (firm B) earns $1.99 ($0.51) each period. Firm A earns $3.42 per period at the uncontested monopoly equilibrium, from $1.10 to $1.80 in the competitive range, and no more than $0.88 per period with a predation strategy.

[99] The "remedy" applied prohibits firm A from expanding production for beyond the maximum quantity ever set by the firm for two periods whenever firm B enters. Firm A also faces a semipermanent price reduction regulation, requiring that all its price reductions last for at least five periods.

markets. Market performance is more anticompetitive (*i.e.*, higher prices and lower market efficiency) when regulatory sanctions are in place, compared to identical markets without the supposed remedies.

Harrison (1988) runs one experiment using the Isaac and Smith parameters, but makes several design changes. The first relaxes the deep pocket advantage of the incumbent. This likely biases the design against observing predation. The more substantive changes involve several levels of prior subject experience in laboratory monopoly and contestable markets, as well as a multi-market feature. The opportunity cost of participating in one market becomes the foregone profits of not participating in the some other market, rather than a simple constant cost factor as in the Isaac and Smith design. Harrison reports evidence of predation. Although, Rutstrom (1985) initiates a careful attempt to reconcile the design changes between the two studies, she fails to replicate the Harrison result in the several treatments considered.[100] The search for predation continues.

Jung, Kagel, and Levin (1991) explore for predatory pricing in an abstract game theoretic setting. The setting is abstract in that each participant is assigned a name (*e.g.*, player A or player B) and provided a 2x2 payoff matrix. No institution is specified. Thus, participants base their decisions on a payoff matrix rather than on explicit *market* incentives (profits are not directly tied to pricing or production decisions). For instance, "player A" chooses "a1" or "a2" without knowing that type A players represent a market entrant and that a1 (a2) corresponds to deciding to enter (not to enter). In fact, it would be difficult for a participant in these games to discern that the games have anything to do with a market. The matrix game experiments are designed to examine the reputation arguments of Kreps and Wilson (1982) and Milgrom and Roberts (1982). While the participants in these games only view the abstract environment, for purposes of summarizing, consider the games using the market terminology

---

[100] The Rutstrom paper is an unpublished manuscript which pre-dates the published version of the Harrison note. The paper does not test *all* of the design changes or the possible combinations of treatments implemented by Harrison. In some sense this is the case of cold fission in the economics laboratory. Until other researchers can replicate the data point, it remains shrouded in uncertainty.

applied by Jung, Kagel and Levin (1991). Each laboratory session includes three monopolists and four entrants in a round of decisions. Each monopolist faces a series of entry threats from the four entrants. The entrants do not know *a priori* whether a monopolist is 'strong' (will punish the entrant by predating) or 'weak.' However, over the course of the round, information on a monopolist's reputation can be collected. Weak monopolists may strategically choose to fight the entrant, to build a reputation of being a strong monopolist, in hopes that other potential entrants decide not to enter. Predatory behavior in the context of the game is documented.

Unfortunately, it is altogether unclear how the abstract game results map into behavior in well-defined market institutions. Further work building the bridge between analysis in such abstract settings and in well-defined institutions is warranted.

Smith and Isaac make a point that is worth repeating. Current theories and experiments of predation fail to acknowledge the importance of capital. Assets of exiting firms will likely be sold, perhaps at a discount, to new or other potential entrants. This severely dilutes the benefits from a predatory strategy.

E. Entry: A Look at the Contestable Markets Hypothesis

Entry prevails as a key variable in antitrust analysis. The laboratory facilitates the study of entry. Most laboratory studies of entry involve tests of the contestable market hypothesis under various conditions in posted-offer markets.[101] The basic structure of the markets examined in these studies includes two firms with identical cost structures that exhibit declining average cost, with each firm owning capacity sufficient to satisfy the entire market. Thus, the conditions for natural monopoly are satisfied. Both strong and weak forms of the contestable markets hypothesis are considered. The former conjectures that the threat of entry is sufficient to assure that competitive equilibrium outcomes are

---

[101] *See also* section D. on predation above.

achieved, while the weaker version predicts that market outcomes will converge toward competitive levels, and lie closer to the competitive solution than to the monopoly prediction.

Coursey, Isaac, and Smith (1984) find that when sunk costs associated with entry are zero, economies of scale in and of themselves are an *ineffective* barrier to entry. In fact, the contestable market hypothesis provides a reasonable prediction of behavior. Four of their six markets quickly converge to the sustainable competitive equilibrium, and the other two gradually approach, but do not reach the competitive range. Over all, the Coursey, Isaac, and Smith data support the weak version of the contestable market hypothesis, yet several of the markets also appear to be consistent with the strong interpretation.

The study includes a *baseline* treatment of markets with a single seller who has the same cost structure as either of the two duopolists in the contestability experimental treatments.[102] Even *without* the threat of entry in the baseline sessions, the unregulated monopolists have difficulty in achieving the monopoly prediction due to buyers strategically withholding demand. Holding back purchases in this design hits the seller at his most profitable units. However, the disciplining effect diminishes over time. Strategic withholding appears at the rate of roughly 9% in the Coursey, Isaac, and Smith monopoly markets, and 1% in the duopoly markets. Thus, the competitive results observed in the duopoly markets arise largely from the contesting discipline of sellers rather than the withholding behavior of buyers. Of course the mere existence of human rather than computerized buyers creates the a credible threat that withholding could occur. Brown-Kruse (1991) examines this using the Coursey, Isaac, and Smith (1984) design, and finds that markets with human, rather than robot, buyers converge faster.

---

[102] A baseline set of market trails is a treatment against which all other treatments are compared. In the Coursey, Isaac, and Smith study, the benchmark against which contestability must be compared is the monopoly case. While the *theoretical* monopoly benchmark is known without conducting any laboratory markets, the *behavioral* benchmark is not.

When the sunk costs of entry are positive, Coursey, Isaac, Luke, and Smith (1984, p. 69) find that support for the strong version of the contestable markets hypothesis weakens, "yet the disciplining power of contestability remains impressive," as sustained monopoly pricing is not observed. Data from all twelve of the markets reported are consistent with the weak form of the contestable markets hypothesis. Although, in contrast to the zero entry cost treatment presented in Coursey, Isaac, and Smith (1984), the dynamics exhibit less of a monotone convergence path in seven of the twelve laboratory markets. No evidence of natural monopoly outcomes, market collapse, or sustainable tacit collusion surface.

Harrison and McKee take issue with (1) the use of human buyers in the Coursey *et al.* (1984) studies instead of computerized perfectly demand revealing buyers that are in closer line with what contestable market theory, as presented in Bamoul, Panzar, and Willig (1982), assumes and (2) the simultaneous nature of price choice when the theory involves a sequencing so that potential entrants can make their entry decision based on the current price set by the incumbent. With respect to the first criticism, Brown-Kruse (1991) points out, the fact that human buyers do not fully reveal their willingness to pay is less of a shortcoming of the experiments than in fact a weakness of the theory to adequately include strategic behavior on the demand side of the market. Taking both points (1) and (2) into account, the Coursey *et al.* experiments can be interpreted as boundary experiments of the contestable market hypothesis, and the theory is in fact fairly robust to the deviations in conditions reported.

When Harrison and McKee examine contestability under the behavioral demand conditions assumed in the theory, and with the Bertrand-Nash sequential choice condition in affect, they find support for the strong version of the contestability hypothesis. However, they fail to compare the two demand conditions *directly* (human versus computerized) or the Bertrand-Nash treatments in isolation, hence compounding the influence of the effects of the conjectures that they advance. In a later study, Harrison, McKee, and Rutstrom (1989) argue that simulation of buyers rather than using human buyers does not

43

significantly affect the results. In fact, both Harrison *et al.* studies digress substantially from the Coursey, *et al.* design.[103] Brown-Kruse (1991) explicitly analyzes the demand conditions with data from experiments designed to address the buyer issue. Her data reveal that *prices are significantly lower when human buyers are present*. The sheer possibility that strategic withholding might occur sufficiently disciplines the market to assure competitive market performance. This supports the findings of Coursey, Isaac, Luke, and Smith (1984), which raised the possibility that buyers' strategic withholding behavior enhances the convergence to the competitive solution. Using the Coursey *et al.* market parameters, Brown-Kruse also tests the contestable markets hypothesis when each duopolist can opt to receive a certain rate of return in an alternate market instead of entering the contestable market. The data reveal no significant difference in adjusted price relative to markets in which the opportunity cost of entry is zero. The effect of sequencing remains to be isolated by holding all other treatment variables constant.

Millner, Pratt, and Reilly (1990) study contestability using a new institution, a real-time posted-offer flow market. In their computerized duopoly markets, sellers may change their price at any point in time, setting a price for a specified *flow* of output per second. The seller with the lowest price for the longest interval makes proportionately more sales the other seller, and costs depend on the rate of production per second. Sellers in this design have identical decreasing marginal cost schedules. Each firm can opt to accept a per second alternate rate of return instead of posting an offer in the flow market. The sunk costs of entry and exit are zero.

Buyers in the flow market are computer simulated to reveal demand fully, purchasing units of the laboratory commodity at their true willingness-to-pay for a given quantity per second. One experimental treatment allows only one seller, who is fully protected from potential entry, and provides

---

[103] Other treatment variables introduced include: different cost and buyer values, a new computerization of a posted-offer market, altered experience levels. The participants in Harrison and McKee are also prescreened for exhibiting risk neutral behavior using a variation of the method employed in Becker, DeGroot, and Marshak (1964).

a benchmark against which to measure the behavior observed in the theoretically contestable laboratory markets.

Under the real-time continuous setting, contestability ostensibly weakens. However, it is difficult to know to what degree the institution actually affects the outcome, for no direct comparison of institutions is made under the same industry parameters. Millner, Pratt, and Reilly find that their data in the theoretically contestable markets fail to converge to any stable equilibrium, including the sustainable Ramsey-efficient competitive equilibrium. Yet, the market performance is significantly more competitive than in the protected monopoly laboratory markets. Contestability increases welfare. Several of the markets exhibit behavior consistent with the unstable price hypothesis, as introduced in Coursey, Isaac, Luke, and Smith: Prices decline while two firms serve the market, until they fall sufficiently so that one firm exits, after which prices increase until entry occurs and the cycle repeats. In the Millner, Pratt, and Reilly experiments, for the periods in which units were traded, the market was contested by both sellers over 70% of the time. The impact of using human buyers in the flow market remains for later study.

All of the reported contestability experiments involve firms with decreasing marginal cost functions, a common condition of natural monopoly. While many antitrust markets that practitioners evaluate do not involve such specialized cost conditions, it is instructive to observe that the threat of entry indeed imposes competitive pressure on behavior, even in the most potentially problematic types of markets. The pressure increases when human buyers replace the perfectly demand-revealing robot buyers that theory assumes. Little laboratory work exists on entry under conditions of constant and increasing marginal cost, and remains an area for future study of interest to the antitrust community. However, preliminary results of (noncontestable) monopoly posted-offer markets under different cost scenarios and simulated buyers in Harrison, McKee, and Rutstrom (1990) suggest that monopolists exert monopoly power most effectively in constant cost industries, followed by decreasing cost and then increasing cost industries. The underlying behavioral difference may stem from the nature of equilibrium in the three price settings. This remains for later research, but may impact the manner in which theorists and antitrust practitioners think about monopoly, even when entry is perfectly suppressed.

F. Facilitating Practices: Elements of the Ethyl Case in the Laboratory

Grether and Plott (1984) designed experiments to parallel the industry structure and practices in the Ethyl case.[104] Both sides of the case agreed on the general structural form of the lead-based antiknock compound industry. Thus, the design of the laboratory market structure was relatively straight-forward. Features of the market included a homogeneous product, inelastic demand, no entry,[105] two large firms, two small firms, low transportation costs, and large buyers.

While the defense and complaint counsels agreed on industry structure, they argued about the conduct that resulted from the following seller practices: (1) most favored nation clauses (guarantees the buyer that no other customer will obtain a lower price for a similar quantity of the good); (2) advanced price announcements; and (3) delivered pricing (price is not contingent on location). Holding the economic parameters constant across experiments, the practices can be introduced, or omitted, so that the effect of the change can be studied. Delivered pricing is present in all of the Grether and Plott laboratory markets.

The FTC counsel contended that uncertainty about rivals firms' actions or reactions encourages competition, and therefore the most favored nation clauses and the advanced price announcements promote collusion. Grether and Plott find that without the practices, the observed prices lie closer to the competitive level than to any other prediction. Introducing both the most favored nation clauses and advanced price announcements leads to a decrease in competition, however the prices lie approximately

---

[104] *Ethyl Corp. v. F.T.C., 729 F.2d 128* (1984).

[105] Entry was unlikely, as the EPA was in the process of phasing out the use of lead in gasoline.

halfway between the predictions of the competitive and Cournot models. The joint maximum, the perfectly collusive outcome, is rejected. Additionally, the most favored nation clause in isolation exerts a *negative* impact on price, the opposite result as argued. However, the price announcements do generate the hypothesized effect of increasing prices.

The conclusions of the Grether and Plott research are consistent with other experimental findings, several of which are discussed above. The application of laboratory analysis to the Ethyl case illustrates how experimental analysis can be useful for increasing our understanding of the prominent elements of complex antitrust situations.

IV. Concluding Remarks

The economics laboratory is an important tool which can enhance understanding of how markets work. The first three decades of laboratory research expands the general knowledge of theoretical industrial organization and applied field analysis relating to antitrust. From this literature, several significant themes suggest directions for policy or topics for further study:

- Institutional form matters more than theory and policy imply. In fact, institutional effects often dominate the effects of structural characteristics of the market. (For instance, the competitive outcome is more robust than economic theory suggests, markets with single sellers do not necessarily lead to monopoly outcomes in certain institutional settings.)

- Standard theories of noncooperative equilibria assume that all market participants have complete information on the payout functions of others, an assumption that is likely violated in most field markets. However, these theories actually predict better in laboratory markets under conditions of private rather than complete information.

47

- Communications of the form the antitrust laws prohibit sometimes lead to collusive outcomes. No support has been found to date that communications in the form of trade press announcements facilitate stable collusion in laboratory markets. Tacit collusion is difficult to coordinate in most settings. When explicit collusion is permitted, the successful implementation of a cartel depends on the form of trading institution: (1) in double-auction markets, collusion usually falls apart; (2) in posted-offer markets, the sellers raise price to the Cournot-Nash level; and (3) in Cournot markets, the sellers sometimes achieve the perfectly collusive outcome.

- Predation is difficult to generate behaviorally in a market context, even under market conditions designed to give the theory its "best shot." Another lesson to be gleaned from research on this topic is that simple game-theoretic models may perform well when tested under the rigid assumptions they dictate however, when the models are imbedded in laboratory market institutions, the models often fail to describe behavior.

- Economies of scale resulting from merger in Cournot laboratory markets are passed on to consumers. The HHI critical values set in the Guidelines are overly restrictive for the markets studied, even when the merging parties do not enjoy economies.

- Market power, when it exists, may be exercised. The effect of institutional form, the nature of capacity, the divisibility of production, and the presence of human buyers are important in determining whether or not it will be. When market power exists and prices are supracompetitive, it is often the case that market power is not exercised fully (in the sense that sellers with power do not withhold production to the extent that theory predicts). Rather, the presence of market power seems to facilitate tacit collusion. Further study is warranted to better understand the relationship of the above variables on the effective exercise of market power, as well as on the incidence of tacit collusion.

Almost all of the results surveyed above involve industries with concentration levels sufficient to "raise significant anticompetitive concern" under the Guidelines (§1.51(b)), when using the Hirfindahl-Hirshman Index (HHI) of concentration to screen for potential horizontal merger cases. Most of the laboratory markets have HHIs of at least 2500 (*e.g.*, four symmetric firms) and many have values of at least 5000 (*e.g.*, duopoly or monopoly). In merger cases litigated by the Federal Trade Commission or the Department of Justice from 1982-1991, roughly 35% of the cases involved industries with HHIs of 2500 or less, 65% of 3333 or less, and 84% of 5000 or less.[106] Thus, the concentration of the markets studied in the laboratory is on average higher than the market concentration in litigated field cases.[107]

It is worthwhile to note that most of the laboratory analysis summarized above omits two features that are critical for antitrust applications: (1) the possibility of entry[108] and (2) the threat of antitrust enforcement.[109] The absence of these factors should bias the data in favor of observing collusive outcomes.[110] Thus, to the extent that collusion is not observed, or when it is, it is unstable, presents

---

[106] *See* Coate (1992).

[107] This may not necessarily be representative of market concentration in cases that fold or settle prior to litigation.

[108] The most notable exceptions include the literature on predation and contestable natural monopolies in the laboratory, *see* §III (D) and (E) *supra*. In particular, little is known currently about entry in laboratory markets with constant or increasing marginal cost environments.

[109] Gerety (1987) incorporates the threat, *see* note 23 *supra*.

[110] By and large, existing laboratory studies and antitrust analysis assume that the structural parameters (*e.g.* costs and demand) of an industry are constant over time. In this regard, both methodologies likely overestimate the ease of tacit collusion if structural shocks are relevant, for the
(continued...)

a strong result: Even *without* the threat of entry or antitrust penalty, many of the markets are still competitive. It is possible to incorporate both of these factors in future laboratory studies.[111] Doing so would likely decrease the incidence of anticompetitive market outcomes, although, it remains to be tested.

Undoubtedly, future laboratory research will bring further progress and perhaps help to reach a consensus on how oligopoly markets work. As laboratory evidence accumulates, it will build an empirical foundation for our understanding of markets.

---

[110](...continued)
shocks would likely make coordination more difficult. It is possible to test directly whether the incidence of supracompetitive pricing decreases when the parameters are not constant.

[111] Another feature that could be important is agency theory. Conn, Young, and Bishop (1991) consider principal-agent theory, but not imbedded in an oligopoly framework.

References

Alger, D. (1986), *Investigating Oligopolies Within the Laboratory*, FTC Bureau of Economics Report.

Alger, D. (1987), "Laboratory Tests of Equilibrium Predictions with Disequilibrium Data," *Review of Economic Studies* 54, 105-145.

Ball, S. and P. Cech (1991), "Subject Pool Selection," Kellogg Graduate School of Management Working Paper 91-42, Northwestern University.

Bamoul, W. J., J. C. Panzar, and R. D. Willig (1982), *Contestable Markets and the Theory of Industry Structure*, San Diego: Harcourt-Brace-Jovanovich.

Benson, B. L. and M. D. Faminow (June 1988), "The Impact of Experience on Prices and Profits in Experimental Duopoly Markets," *Journal of Economic Behavior and Organization*, 9, 345-365.

Binger B. R., E. Hoffman, G. D. Libecap, and K. M. Schachat (1992), "An Experimetric Study of the Cournot Model," University of Arizona Working Paper 92-13.

Bolton, G. E. (December 1991), "A Comparative Model of Bargaining: Theory and Evidence," *American Economic Review*, 81(5), 1096-1136.

Bork, R. H. (1978), *The Antitrust Paradox*, New York: Free Press.

Brown-Kruse, J. L. (March 1986), "Laboratory Tests of Buyer Rationing Rules in Bertrand-Edgeworth Duopolies," Revised Manuscript, June 1990, University of Colorado.

Brown-Kruse, J. L. (Spring 1991), "Contestability in the Presence of an Alternative Market: An Experimental Examination," *RAND Journal of Economics*, 22(1), 136-147.

Brown-Kruse, J. L., M. B. Cronshaw, and D. J. Schenk (January 1993), "Theory and Experiments on Spatial Competition," *Economic Inquiry*, 31(1), 139-165.

Brown-Kruse, J., S. Rassenti, S. S. Reynolds, and V. L. Smith (1987), "Bertrand-Edgeworth Competition in Experimental Markets," University of Arizona Discussion Paper 87-12, forthcoming in *Econometrica*.

Burns, P. (1985), "Experience and Decision Making: A comparison of Students and Businessmen in a Simulated Progressive Auction," *Research in Experimental Economics, Volume 3*, V. L. Smith, ed., Greenwich, CT: JAI Press, 139-157.

Carlson, J. A. (January 1967), "The Stability of An Experimental Market With a Supply-Response Lag," *Southern Economic Journal*, 33(3), 305-321.

Carlton, D. W. and J. M. Perloff (1989), *Modern Industrial Organization*, Glenview, IL: Scott, Foresman/Little, Brown Higher Education.

Chamberlin, E. (1948), "An Experimental Imperfect Market," *Journal of Political Economy*, 56(2), 95-108.

Camerer, C. F. (December 1987), "Do Biases in Probability Judgement Matter in Markets? Experimental Evidence," *American Economic Review*, 77(5), 981-997.

Camerer, C. F., G. Lowenstein, and M. Weber (1989), "The Curse of Knowledge in Economic Settings: An Experimental Analysis," *Journal of Political Economy*, 97(5), 1232-1254.

Coate, M. B. (1992), "Economics, the Guidelines and the Evolution of Merger Policy," *Antitrust Bulletin*, Winter, 997-1024.

Coate, M. B., A. N. Kleit, and R. Bustamante (1993), "Fight, Fold, or Settle?: Modeling the Reaction to FTC Merger Challenges," FTC Working Paper 200.

Conn, D., S. M. Young, and R. A. Bishop (1991), "Testing Principal-Agent Theory: A Framework for Analysis and Results From Three Experiments in a Non-Stochastic Setting," University of Southern California School of Business.

Coursey, D., R. M. Isaac, R. M. Luke and V. L. Smith (Spring 1984), "Market Contestability in the Presence of Sunk Costs," *RAND Journal of Economics*, 69-84.

Coursey, D., R. M. Isaac, and V. L. Smith (April 1984), "Natural Monopoly and Contested Markets," *Journal of Law and Economics*, 27, 91-113.

Cox, J. C., Dinkin, and V. L. Smith (1993), "Endogenous Entry and Exit in Common Value Auctions," University of Arizona Department of Economics Working Paper.

Cox, J. C. and R. M. Isaac (1986), "Experimental Economics and Experimental Psychology: Ever the Twain Shall Meet," *Economic Psychology: Intersections in Theory and Application*, A. J. and H. W. MacFadyen, eds., Elsevier Science Publishers B. V. (North-Holland).

Cox, J. C. and R. L. Oaxaca (1990), Using Laboratory Market Experiments to Evaluate Econometric Estimators of Structural Models," Manuscript, University of Arizona.

Cox, J. C., B. Roberson, and V. L. Smith (1982), "Theory and Behavior of Single Object Auctions," *Research in Experimental Economics, Volume 2*, V. L. Smith, ed., Greenwich, CT: JAI Press, 1-43.

Davidson, C. and R. Deneckere (1990), "Excess Capacity and Collusion," *International Economic Review*, 31(3), 521-541.

Davis, D. D., G. W. Harrison, and A. W. Williams (1993), "Convergence to Nonstationary Competitive Equilibria: An Experimental Analysis," *Journal of Economic Behavior and Organization*, forthcoming.

Davis, D. D. and C. A. Holt (1991), "Capacity Asymmetries, Market Power, and Mergers in Laboratory Markets with Posted Prices," Manuscript, Virginia Commonwealth University.

Davis, D. D., C. A. Holt, and A. P. Villamil (1990), "Supra-Competitive Prices and Market Power in Posted-Offer Experiments," BEBR Working Paper 90-1648, University of Illinois Urbana-Champaign.

Davis, D. D. and A. Williams (1986), "The Effects of Rent Asymmetries in Posted-offer Markets," *Journal of Economic Behavior and Organization*, 7, 303-316.

Davis, D. D. and A. Williams (April 1990a), "Convergence to Nonstationary Competitive Equilibria: An Experimental Analysis," Manuscript, Indiana University.

Davis, D. D. and A. Williams (1990b), "Market Power and the Institutional Asymmetry of the Posted-offer Trading Institution," *Economic Letters*, 34(3), 211-214.

Davis, D. D. and A. Williams (1991), "The Hayek Hypothesis in Experimental Auctions: Institutional Effects and Market Power," *Economic Inquiry*, 29, 261-274.

Demsetz, H. (1973), *The Market Concentration Doctrine*, Washington, D.C.: American Enterprise Institute.

Deneckere, R. and D. Kovenock (1989) "Capacity-Constrained Price Competition when Unit Costs Differ," CMSEMS Discussion Paper 861, Northwestern University.

Dolbear, F. T., L. B. Lave, and G. Bowman (1966), "Collusion in Oligopoly: An Experiment of Numbers and Information," *Quarterly Journal of Economics*, 82(2), 240-259.

Durham, Y., S. Rassenti, V. L. Smith, M. Van Boening, and N. T. Wilcox (1993), "Can Core Allocations Be Achieved in Avoidable Fixed Cost Environments Using Two-Part Price Competition?" presented at the Western Economic Association Meetings, Lake Tahoe, NV, June 22.

Dyer, D. and J. H. Kagel (1992), "Experienced Bidders in Common Value Auctions: Behavior in the Laboratory versus the Natural Habitat," Manuscript, Department of Economics, University of Pittsburgh, presented in the FTC Bureau of Economics Seminar Series, Spring 1992.

Easley, D. and J. Ledyard (1988), "Theories of Price Formation and Exchange in Oral Auctions," Manuscript, California Institute of Technology.

Fama, E. F., and A. B. Laffer (1972), "The Number of Firms and Competition," *American Economic Review*, 62, 670-674.

Fouraker, L. and S. Siegel (1963), *Bargaining Behavior*, New York, McGraw-Hill.

Friedman, D. (March 1984), "On the Efficiency of Double-Auction Markets," *American Economic Review*, 74(1), 60-72.

Friedman, D. (1991), "A Simple Testable Model of Double-Auction Markets," *Journal of Economic Behavior and Organization*, 15, 47-70.

Friedman, D. and J. Ostroy (September 1991), "Competitivity in Auction Markets: An Experimental and Theoretical Investigation," Manuscript, University of California, Santa Cruz.

Friedman, J. W. (1967), "An Experimental Study of Cooperative Duopoly," *Econometrica*, 379-397.

Friedman, J. W. and A. C. Hoggatt (1980), "An Experiment in Noncooperative Oligopoly," *Research in Experimental Economics, Supplement 1*, Greenwich, CT: JAI Press.

Garvin, S. and J. Kagel (December 1990), "An Experimental Investigation of Limit Entry Pricing," Manuscript, University of Pittsburgh.

Gerety, V. E. (1987), *Formation and Control of Collusion in a Sealed Offer Market: An Experimental Examination*, University of Arizona Ph.D. Dissertation.

Grether, D. (1980), "Bayes Rule as a Descriptive Model: The Representativeness Heuristic," *Quarterly Journal of Economics*, 95, 537-557.

Grether, D. (1992), "Testing Bayes Rule and the Representativeness Heuristic: Some Experimental Evidence," *Journal of Behavior and Organization*, 17(1), 31-57.

Grether, D. and C. Plott (October 1984), "The Effects of Market Practices in Oligopolistic Markets: An Experimental Examination of the Ethyl Case," *Economic Inquiry*, 22, 479-507.

Harrison, G. (1987), "Experimental Evaluation of the Contestable Markets Hypothesis," *Public Regulation: New Perspectives on Institutions and Policies*, E. E. Bailey, ed., Cambridge: MIT Press, 191-225.

Harrison, G. (1988), "Predatory Pricing in a Multiple Market Experiment," *Journal of Economic Behavior and Organization*, 9, 405-417.

Harrison G. and M. McKee (Spring 1985), "Monopoly Behavior, Decentralized Regulation, and Contestable Markets: An Experimental Evaluation," *RAND Journal of Economics*, 16(1), 51-69.

Harrison, G., M. McKee, and E. E. Rutstrom (1990), "Experimental Evaluation of Institutions of Monopoly Restraint," *Advances in Behavioral Economics, Volume II*, Green and Kagel, eds., Norwood, N.J.: Ablex, 54-94.

Hayek, F. A. (September 1945), "The Use of Knowledge in Society," *American Economic Review*, 35(4), 519-530.

Hoffman, E. and C. R. Plott (1981), "The Effect of Intertemporal Speculation on the Outcomes in Seller Posted Offer Auction Markets," *Quarterly Journal of Economics*, 96, 223-241.

Hoffman, E. and M. Spitzer (April 1982), "The Coase Theorem: Some Experimental Tests," *Journal of Law and Economics*, 25, 73-98.

Hoggatt, A. C. (July 1959), "An Experimental Business Game," *Behavioral Science*, 4, 192-203.

Hoggatt, A. C., J. W. Friedman, and S. Gill (1967), "Price Signaling in Experimental Oligopoly," *American Economic Review*, 66(2), 261-266.

Holt, C. A. (June 1985), "An Experimental Test of the Consistent-Conjectures," *American Economic Review*, 75, 314-325.

Holt, C. A. (October 1989), "The Exercise of Market Power in Laboratory Experiments," *Journal of Law and Economics*, 32, S107-S130.

Holt, C. A. (1991), "Industrial Organization: A Survey of Laboratory Research," *Handbook of Experimental Economics*, Princeton University Press.

Holt, C. A. and D. D. Davis (December 1990), "The Effects of Non-Binding Price Announcements on Posted-Offer Markets," *Economic Letters*, 34, 307-310.

Holt, C. A., L. W. Langan and A. P. Villamil (1986), "Market Power in Oral Double-auctions," *Economic Inquiry*, 24, 107-123.

Hong, J. and Plott, C. (1982), "Rate Filing Policies for Inland Water Transportation," *Bell Journal of Economics*, 13(1), 1-19.

Hurwicz, L. (1972), "The Design of Mechanisms for Resource Allocation," *American Economic Review, Papers and Proceedings*, 63, 1-30.

Isaac, R. M. (July 1983), "Laboratory Experimental Economics as a Tool in Public Policy Analysis," *The Social Science Journal*, 20(3), 45-58.

Isaac, R. M. (1990), "Laboratory Studies of Monopoly and Conspiracy," Manuscript, University of Arizona.

Isaac, R. M. and C. Plott (1981), "The Opportunity for Conspiracy in Restraint of Trade: An Experimental Study," *Journal of Economic Behavior and Organization*, 2, 1-30.

Isaac, R. M., R. L. Oaxaca, and S. S. Reynolds (1988), "Competition and Pricing in the Arizona Gasoline Market," University of Arizona Discussion Paper 88-16.

Isaac, R. M., V. Ramey, and A. Williams (1984), "The Effects of Market Organization on Conspiracies in Restraint of Trade," *Journal of Economic Behavior and Organization*, 5, 191-222.

Isaac, R. M. and S. S. Reynolds (1989), "Appropriability and Market Structure in a Stochastic Invention Model," *Quarterly Journal of Economics*, 103, 647-672.

Isaac, R. M. and S. S. Reynolds (1990), "Two or Four Firms: Does it Matter?" Manuscript, University of Arizona.

Isaac, R. M. and V. L. Smith (1985), "In Search of Predatory Pricing," *Journal of Political Economy*, 93, 320-345.

Isaac, R. M. and J. Walker (1985), Information and Conspiracy in Sealed Bid Auctions," *Journal of Economic Behavior and Organization*, 6, 139-159.

Jung, Y. J., J. H. Kagel, and D. Levin (1991), "On the Existence of Predatory Pricing: An Experimental Study of Reputation and Entry Deterrence in the Chain-Store Game," Manuscript, University of Pittsburgh.

Kagel, J. and A. Roth, eds.(1991), *Handbook of Experimental Economics*, Princeton University Press.

Ketcham, J., V. L. Smith, and A. Williams (1984), "A Comparison of Posted-Offer and Double-Auction Pricing Institutions," *Review of Economic Studies*, 51, 595-614.

Kirkwood, J. (1981), "Antitrust Implications of Recent Experimental Literature on Collusion," in *Strategy, Predation, and Antitrust Analysis*, S. Salop, ed., FTC Bureau of Economics Report.

Kreps, D. and J. Scheinkman (1983), "Quantity Precommitment and Bertrand Competition Yield Cournot Outcomes," *Bell Journal of Economics*, 14,326-337.

Kreps, D. and R. Wilson (1982), "Reputation and Imperfect Information," *Journal of Economic Theory*, 27, 253-279.

Ketcham, J., V. L. Smith, and A. Williams (1984), "A Comparison of Posted-Offer and Double-auction Pricing Institutions," *Review of Economic Studies*, 51(4), 595-614.

King, R., V. L. Smith, A. Williams, and M. Van Boening (forthcoming), "The Robustness of Bubbles and Crashes in Experimental Stock Markets," *Nonlinear Dynamics and Evolutionary Economics*, I. Prigogine, R. H. Day, and P. Chen, eds., Oxford: Oxford University Press.

Kitch, E. W., ed. (1983), "The Fire of Truth: A Remembrance of Law and Economics at Chicago, 1932-1970," *Journal of Law and Economics* 26, 163-234.

Levin, D. (April 1988), "Stackelberg, Cournot, and Collusive Monopoly: Performance and Welfare Comparison," *Economic Inquiry*, 26, 317-330.

McCabe, K., S. Rassenti, and V. L. Smith (1989), "Lakatos and Experimental Economics," University of Arizona Discussion Paper 89-24.

McGee, J. S. (1971), *In Defense of Industrial Concentration*, New York: Praeger Publishers Incorporated.

Mestelman, S., D. Welland, and D. J. Welland (June 1987), "Advance Production in Posted-Offer Markets," *Review of Economic Studies*, 55(4), 641-654.

Mestelman, S. and D. J. Welland (October 1988), "Advance Production in Experimental Markets," *Journal of Economic Behavior and Organization*, 8, 249-264.

Milgrom, P. and J. Roberts (1982), "Predation, Reputation, and Entry Deterrence," *Journal of Economic Theory*, 27, 280-312.

Miller, R., C. Plott, and V. L. Smith (November 1977), "Intertemporal Competitive Equilibrium: An Empirical Study of Speculation," *Quarterly Journal of Economics*, 91, 599-624.

Millner, E. L., M. D. Pratt, and R. J. Reilly (1990), "Contestability in Real-Time Experimental Flow Markets," *RAND Journal of Economics*, 21(4), 584-599.

Morrison, C. C. and H. Kamarei (1990), "Some Experimental Testing of the Cournot-Nash Hypothesis in Small Group Rivalry Situations," *Journal of Economic Behavior and Organization*, 13(2), 213-231.

Plott, C. (1982), "Industrial Organization Theory and Experimental Economics," *Journal of Economic Literature*, 20(4), 1485-1527.

Plott, C. (1987) "Some Policy Applications of Experimental Methods," *Laboratory Experimentation in Economics*, A. E. Roth, ed. Cambridge: Cambridge University Press, 193-219.

Plott, C. (1989), "An Updated Review of Industrial Organization: Applications of Experimental Methods," *Handbook of Industrial Organization, Volume II*, eds. R. Schmalensee and R. D. Willig, Elsevier Science Publishers.

Plott, C. and V. L. Smith (1978), "Experimental Examination of Two Exchange Institutions," *Review of Economic Studies*, 45(1), 133-153.

Posner, R. A. (1976), *Antitrust Law*, Chicago: The University of Chicago Press.

Rassenti, S. J., S. S. Reynolds, and V. L. Smith (October 1989), "Cotenancy and Competition in an Experimental Auction Market for Natural Gas Pipeline Networks," Manuscript, University of Arizona.

Rutstrom, E. E. (December 1985), "In Search of a Reconciliation of Results in Predatory Pricing Experiments," Manuscript, University of South Carolina.

Sargent, T. J. (1992) "Milton, Money, and Mischief," presented at the Western Economic Association Meetings, San Fransisco, CA, Forthcoming, *Economic Inquiry*.

Scherer, F. M. (1980), *Industrial Market Structure and Economic Performance*, Second Edition, Boston: Houghton Mifflin Company.

Schmalensee, R. (January 1976), " An Experimental Study of Expectation Formation," *Econometrica*, 44, 17-41.

Sherman, R. (April 1976), "An Experiment on the Persistence of Price Collusion," *Southern Economic Journal*, 26, 489-495.

Smith, A. (1937), originally 1776, *The Wealth of Nations*, New York: Random House, Modern Library Edition.

Smith, V. L. (1962), "An Experimental Study of Competitive Market Behavior," *Journal of Political Economy*, 70(2), 111-137.

Smith, V. L. (1964), Effect of Market Organization on Competitive Equilibrium," *Quarterly Journal of Economics*, 78(2), 181-201.

Smith, V.L. (1965), "Experimental Auction Markets and the Walrasian Hypothesis," *Journal of Political Economy*, 73(4), 387-393.

Smith, V. L. (1967), Experimental Studies of Discrimination Versus Competition in Sealed-Bid Auction Markets," *Journal of Business*, 40, 56-84.

Smith, V. L. (1976a), "Bidding and Auctioning Institutions: Experimental Results," *Bidding and Auctioning for Procurement and Allocation*, Y. Amihaud, ed., New York: New York University Press, 43-64.

Smith, V. L. (1976b), "Induced Value Theory," *American Economic Review*, 66(2), 274-279.

Smith, V. L. (1981a), "An Empirical Study of Decentralized Institutions of Monopoly Restraint," *Essays in Contemporary Fields of Economics in Honor of Emanuel T. Weiler (1914-1979)*, G. Horwich and J. Quirk, eds., Purdue University Press, 83-106.

Smith, V. L. (1981b), "Theory, Experiment, and Antitrust Policy," *Strategy, Predation, and Antitrust Analysis*, ed. S. Salop, FTC Bureau of Economics Report.

Smith, V. L. (April 1982a), "Markets as Economizers of Information: Experimental Examination of the 'Hayek Hypothesis'," *Economic Inquiry*, 20, 165-179.

Smith, V. L. (December 1982b), "Microeconomic Systems as an Experimental Science," *American Economic Review*, 72, 923-955.

Smith, V. L. (1982c), "Reflections on Some Experimental Market Mechanisms for Classical Environments," *Choice Models for Buyer Behavior: Research in Marketing*, Supplement 1, Greenwich, CT: JAI Press, 13-47.

Smith, V. L. (1987), "Experimental Methods in Economics," *The New Palgrave*, volume 1, J. Eatwell, M. Milgate, and P. Newman, eds., New York, NY: W. W. Norton and Company, 94-111.

Smith, V. L. (1988/1989), "New Directions for Economics," *Journal of Business Administration, Special Issue: Future Directions for Economics*, 18(1,2), 41-52 (an earlier version was presented on February 28, 1986 at the first official meeting of the Economic Science Association, Tucson, Arizona).

Smith, V. L. (Winter 1989), "Theory, Experiment and Economics," *Journal of Economic Perspectives*, 3(1), 151-169.

Smith, V. L. (1990), "Experimental Economics: Behavioral Lessons for Microeconomic Theory and Policy," Nancy L. Schwartz Memorial Lecture, Kellogg Graduate School of Management, Northwestern University.

Smith, V. L. (1991a), *Papers in Experimental Economics*, Cambridge: Cambridge University Press.

Smith, V. L. (1991b), "Game Theory and Experimental Economics: Beginning and Early Influences," University of Arizona Working Paper 91-5.

Smith, V. L. (1991c), "Rational Choice: The Contrast between Economics and Psychology," *Journal of Political Economy*, 99, 877-897.

Smith, V. L. (July 1992), "Experimental Economics: Evaluating Microeconomic Policies and Institutional Designs," Manuscript, presented in the Economic Analysis Group Seminar Series, Department of Justice Antitrust Division.

Smith, V. L. (Winter 1993), "Economics in the Laboratory," *Journal of Economic Perspectives*, forthcoming.

Smith, V. L. and J. Walker (April 1993), "Monetary Rewards and Decision Cost in Experimental Economics," *Economic Inquiry*, 31, 245-261.

Smith, V. L. and A. Williams (June 1981), "On Nonbinding Price Controls in a Competitive Market," *American Economic Review*, 71(3), 467-474.

Smith, V. L. and A. Williams (September 1982), "The Effects of Rent Asymmetries in Experimental Auction Markets," *Journal of Economic Behavior and Organization*.

Smith, V. L. and A. Williams (September 1989), "The Boundaries of Competitive Price Theory: Convergence, Expectations, and Transaction Costs," *Advances in Behavioral Economics, Volume 1*, L. Green and J. Kagel, eds., Norwood, N.J.:Ablex, 31-53.

Smith, V. L., A. Williams, K. Bratton, and M. Vannoni (1982), "Competitive Market Institutions: Double-Auctions versus Sealed Bid-Offer Auctions," *American Economic Review*, 72(1), 58-77.

U.S. Department of Justice (1984), "Merger Guidelines," *Federal Register*, 49, 26284.

U.S. Department of Justice and Federal Trade Commission (April 2, 1992), "Horizontal Merger Guidelines," *Antitrust Trade and Regulation Report*, 1559.

Van Boening, M. V. and N. Wilcox (1992), "A Fixed Cost Exception to the Hayek Hypothesis," presented at the Economic Science Association Meetings, October 24.

Vickrey, W. (1961), "Counterspeculation, Auctions, and Competitive Sealed Tenders," *Journal of Finance*, 16(1), 3-37.

Wellford, C. P. (1989), "Price Dynamics and Expectations in the Cobweb Model: An Experimental Analysis," University of Arizona Discussion Paper 89-15, Revised Manuscript, 1991, Federal Trade Commission.

Wellford, C. P. (1990), "Horizontal Mergers: Concentration and Performance," Chapter 2 of University of Arizona Ph.D. Dissertation.

Wilcox, N. T. (1989), "Well-Defined Loss Metrics and the Situations that Demand Them," presented at the Economic Science Association Meetings, Tucson, AZ, October 28-29.

Wilcox, N. T. (1992), "Incentives, Complexity, and Time Allocation in a Decision-Making Environment," presented at the Public Choice/Economic Science Association Meetings, New Orleans, LA, March 27-29.

Williams, F. (1973), "The Effect of Market Organization on Competitive Equilibrium: The Multiunit Case," *Review of Economic Studies*, 40(1), 97-113.

Williams, A. (1979), "Intertemporal Competitive Equilibrium: On Further Experimental Results," *Research in Experimental Economics, Volume 1*, V. L. Smith, ed., Greenwich, CT: JAI Press, 255-278.

Wilson, R. (1987), "On Equilibria of Bid-Ask Markets," *Arrow and the Ascent of Economic Theory: Essays in honor of Kenneth J. Arrow*, G. Feiwel, ed., London: McMillan Press, 375-414.

Figure 1 [*]
Double Auction 2DA 24

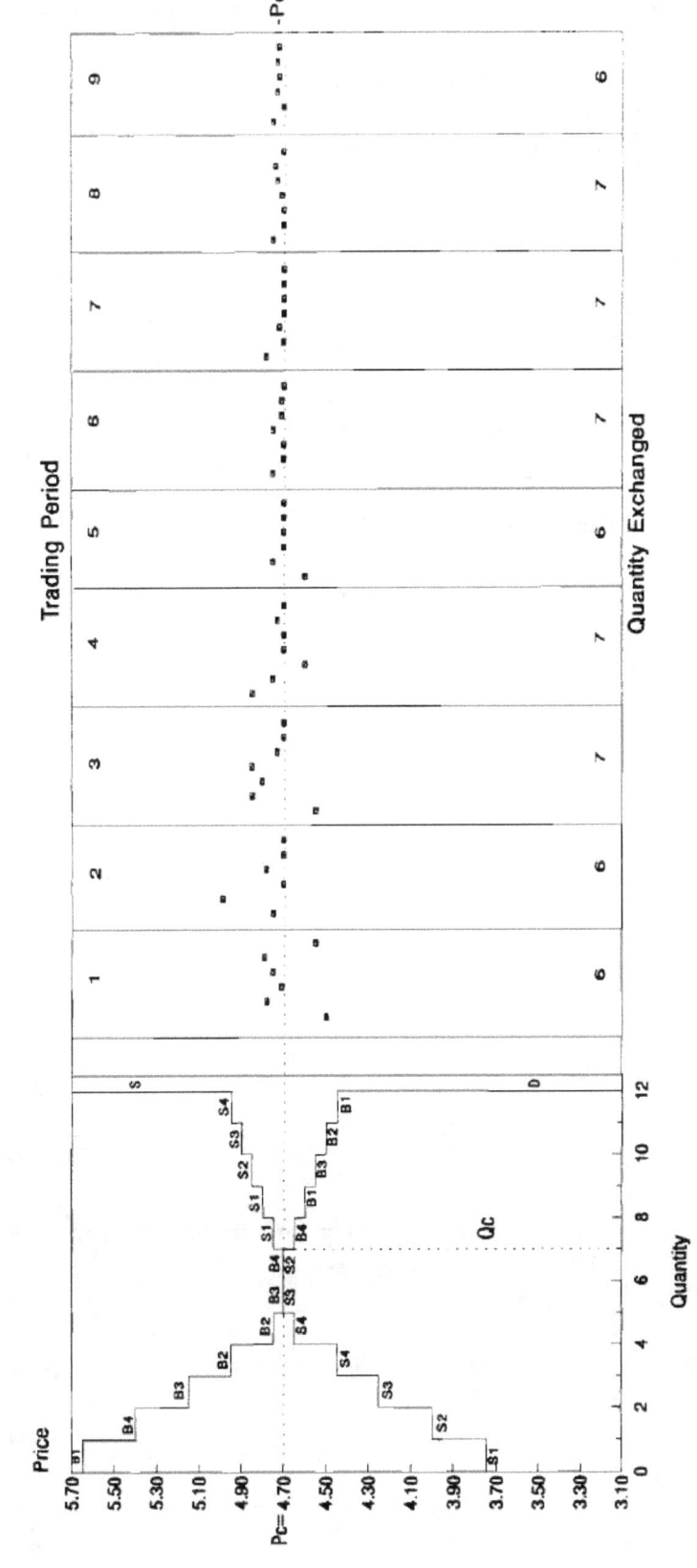

*Source: Ketcham, Smith, and Williams (1984).

Figure 2*

Double Auction Monopoly M1x

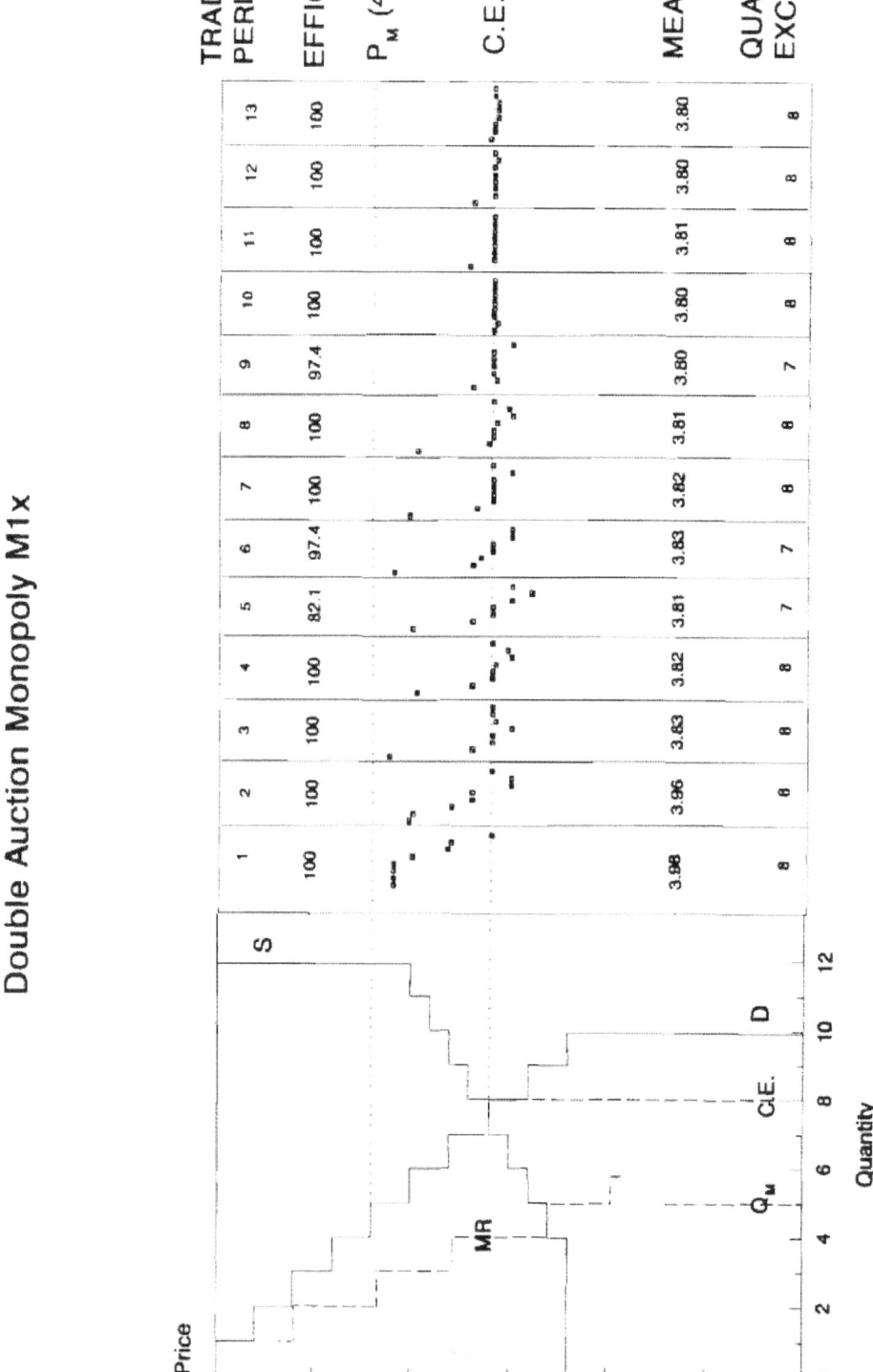

* Source: Smith and Williams (1989).

Figure 3*

Posted Offer PO17ixs

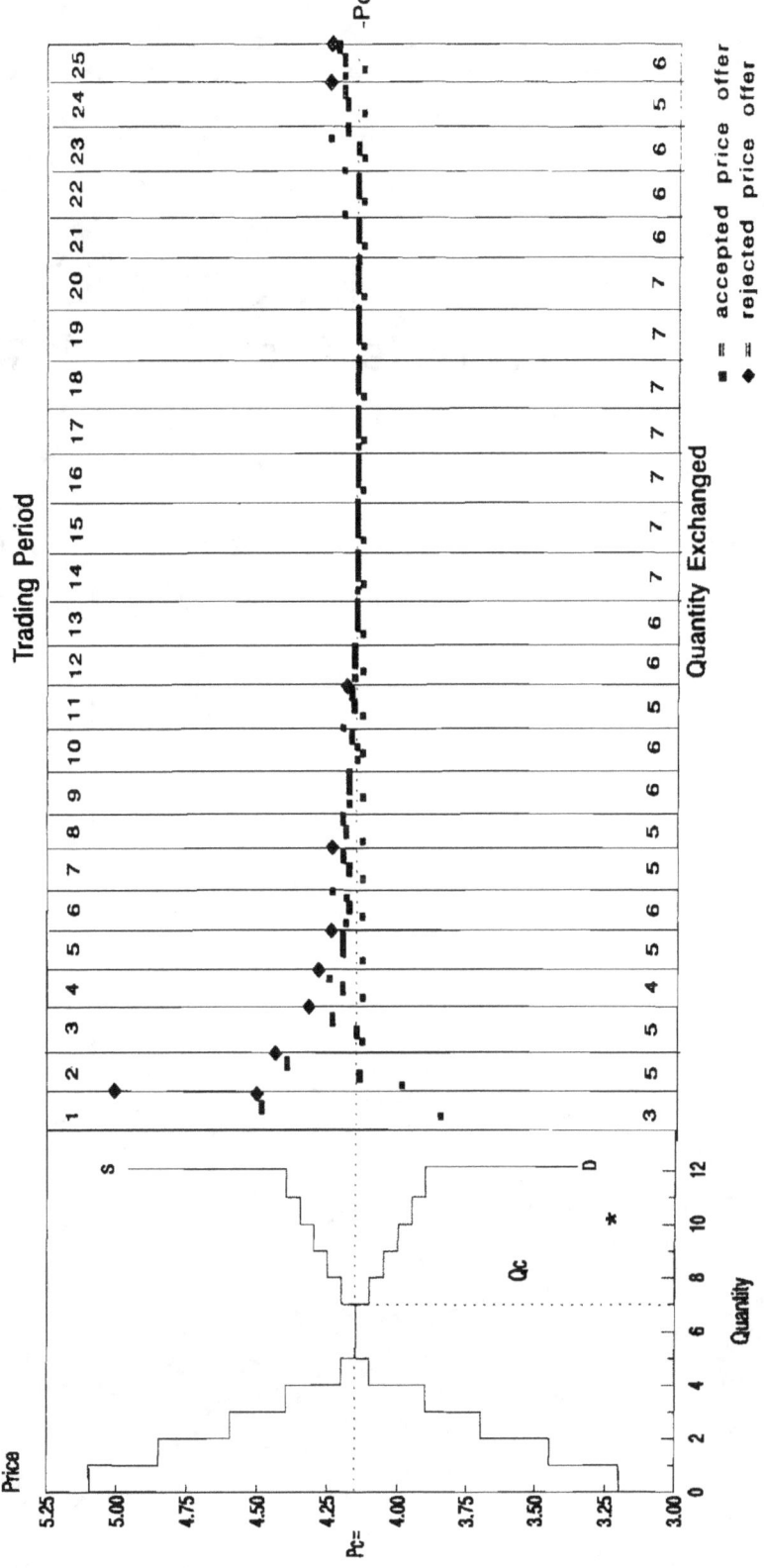

Source: Ketcham, Smith, and Williams (1984).

Figure 4[*]
Double Auction IIpda43

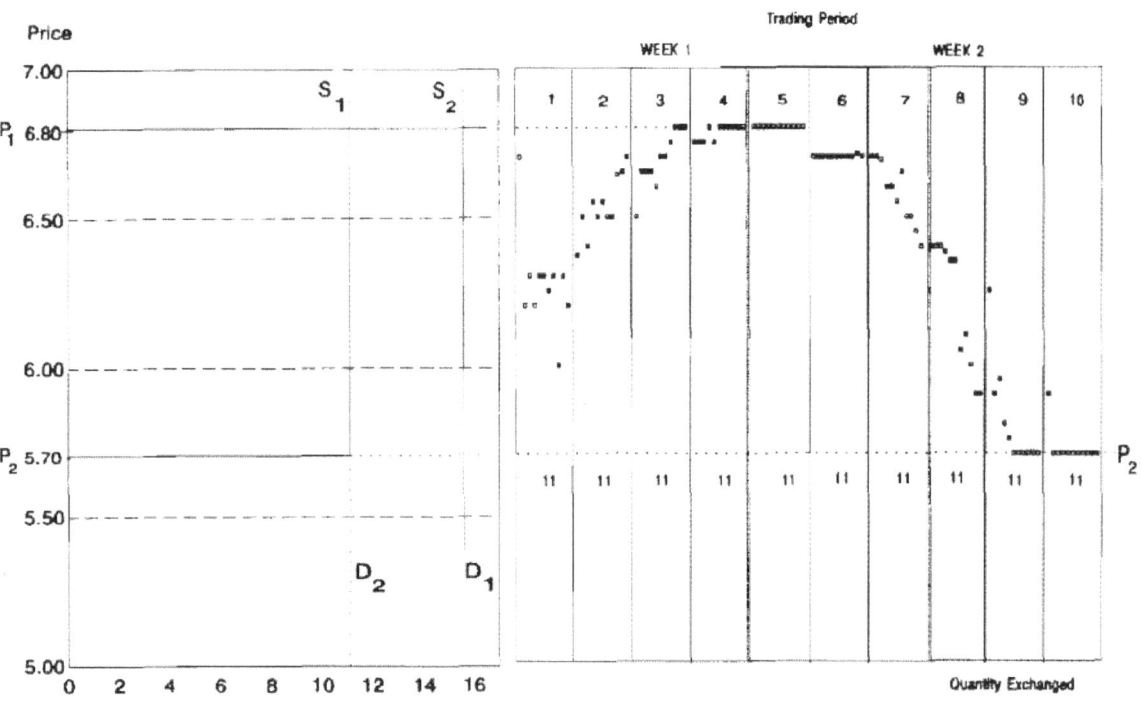

*Source: Smith (1982a).

Figure 5 [*]
Market Power Design

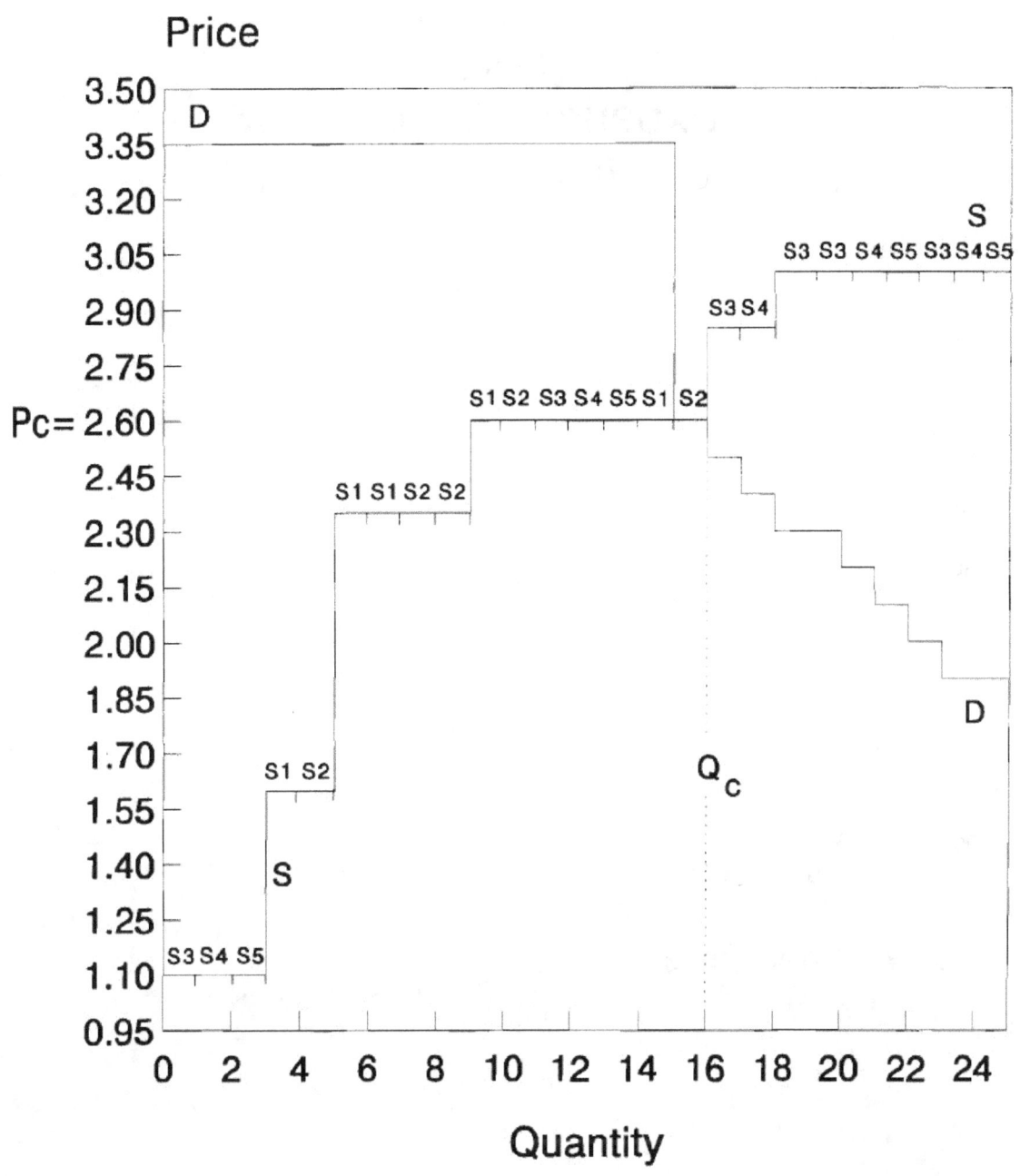

[*]Source: Holt, Langan, and Villamil (1986).

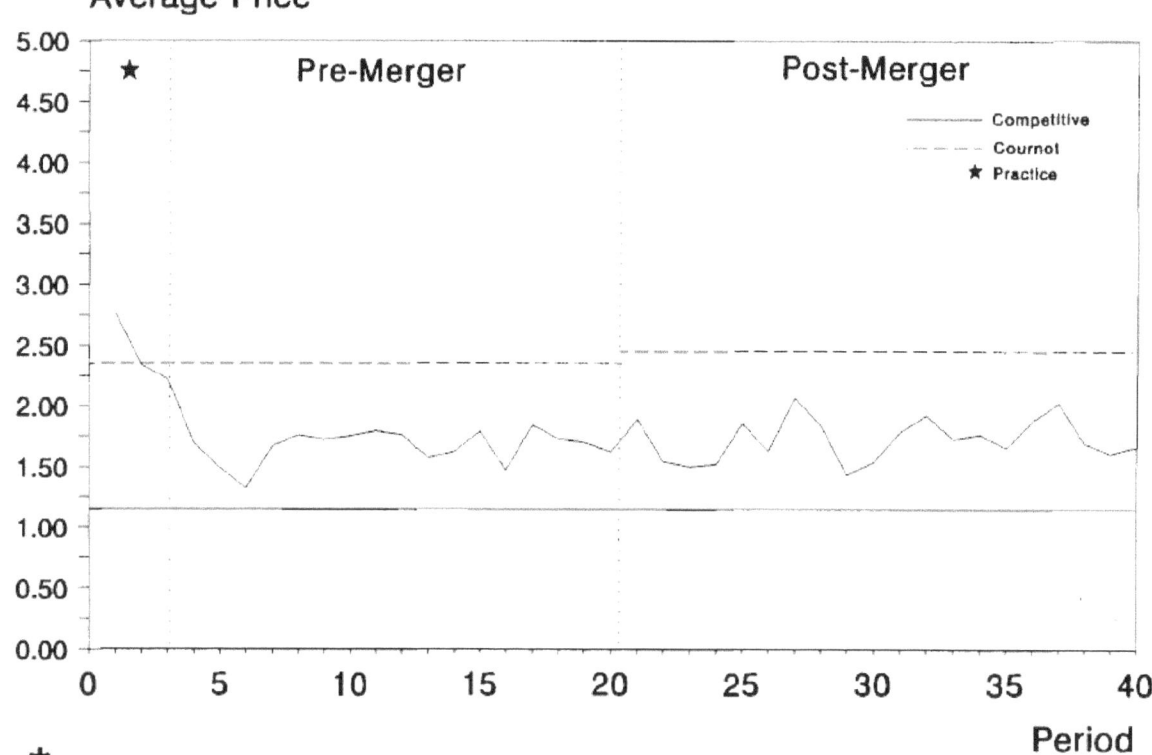

Figure 6[*]
Experiments 501 - 505
(No Economies)

*Source: Wellford (1992).

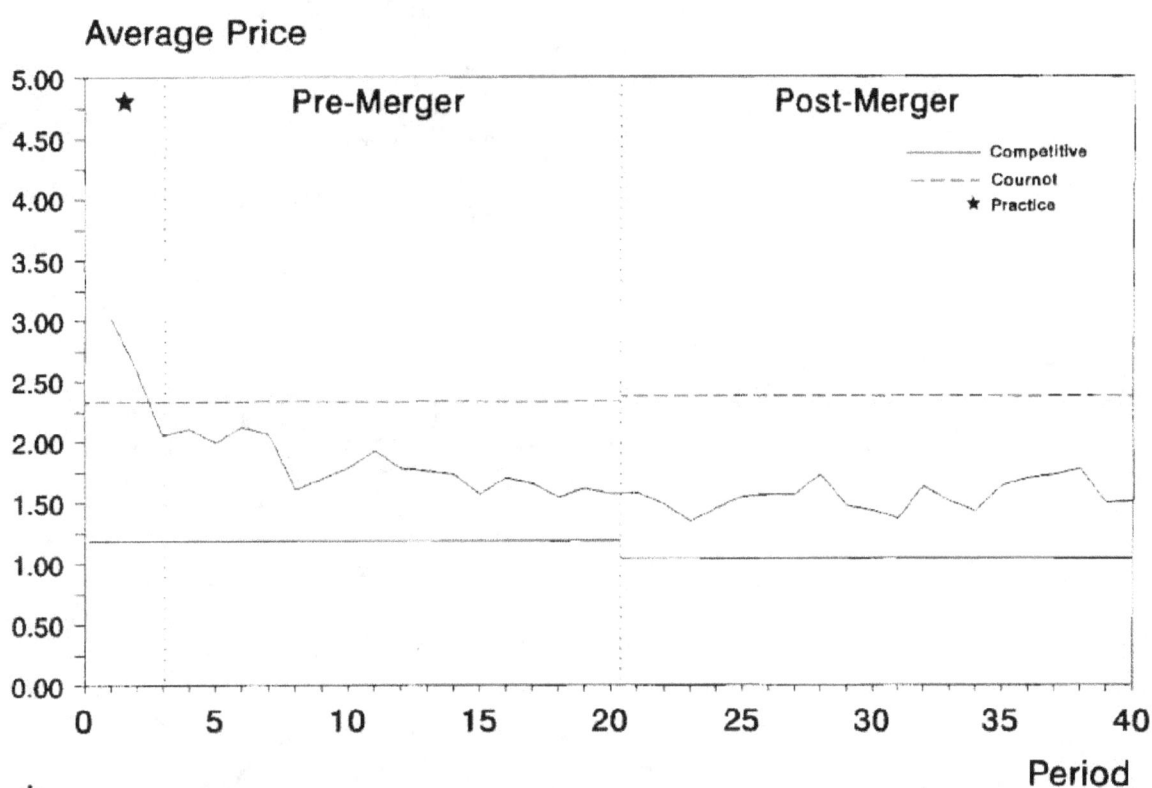

Figure 7[*]
Experiments 506 - 510
(With Economies)

*Source: Wellford (1992).

Figure 8[*]

Cost and Demand Parameters
Predatory Pricing Experiments

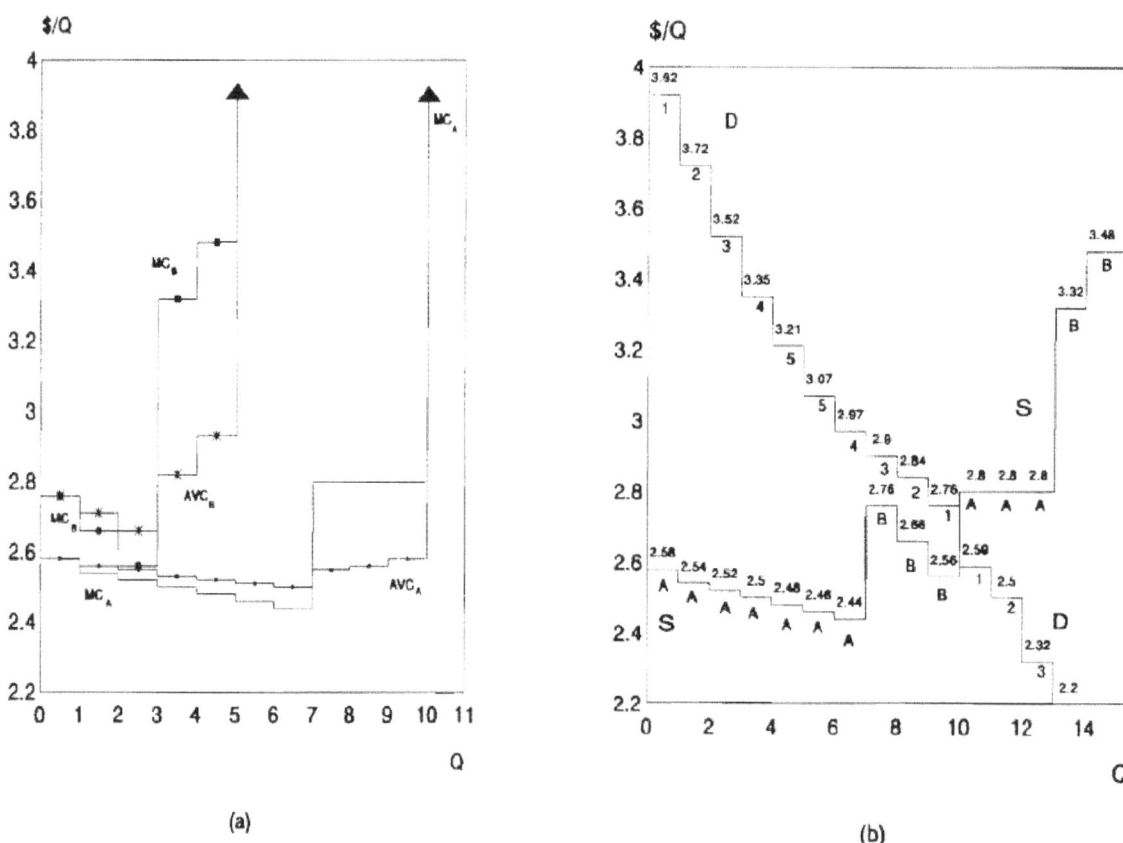

(a)

(b)

[*]
Source: Isaac and Smith (1985).

Table 1

Percentage of Period 21 Market Quantity Observations
Supporting a Particular Equilibrium Concept
Under Private Information Conditions
in Fouraker and Siegel's Cournot Markets[*]
(*Complete Information Treatments in Parentheses*)

Equilibrium Concept	Duopoly	Triopoly
Joint Max	0.00	0.00
	(31.25)	(0.00)
Cournot	87.50	81.82
	(46.87)[†]	(45.45)
CE	12.50	18.18
	(21.88)[†]	(54.55)

[*] Compiled from pages 131, 134, 140, and 141.

[†] One observation is equidistant between the Cournot and the Competitive Equilibrium (CE). Each of the two equilibria is given equal weight of 0.5 for this observation in the calculation of the percentages.

Table 2

Percentage of Period 14 Market Price Observations
Supporting a Particular Equilibrium Concept
Under Private Information Conditions
in Fouraker and Siegel's Bertrand Markets[*]
(*Complete Information Treatments in Parentheses*)

Equilibrium Concept	Duopoly	Triopoly
Joint Max	0.00	0.00
	(35.29)	(0.00)
Bertrand	100.00	100.00
	(64.71)	(100.00)

[*] Compiled from pages 174, 177, 181, and 183.

Table 3

Laboratory Studies of Market Power

Study	Institution	Excess Capacity at CE	Sellers	Buyers	Trials	Market Performance	Average Market Efficiency
Holt, Langan, and Villamil (1986)	DA	Yes	5†	5	3, 2x	Two of the markets converge to the CE, the others converge to a price slightly above the CE price. On average, the deviations from the CE are observed with higher frequency when the sellers have previous experience in the PO institution.	100% (in period 8)
Davis and Williams (1991)	DA	Yes	5†	5	2, 2x	Supracompetitive prices are observed, but cannot be explained by the strategic withholding of quantity by sellers with theoretical market power.	98%
Friedman and Ostroy (1991)	DA with Divisible Units	In Some Markets	4	4	5x	Strategic withholding is negligible. By strategically misrepresenting their true valuations, market agents unintentionally achieve the competitive outcome.	> 95%
Davis, Holt, and Villamil (1990)	PO	Yes	either 2 or 3	*	2, 2x 2, 2x	Static market power leads to observed supracompetitive prices. Median price is less than (exceeds) the mixed strategy Nash equilibrium prediction in the duopoly (triopoly) markets. Some evidence of tacit collusion exists, but it is imperfect, with price lower than the shared monopoly outcome.	NR
Davis and Williams (1990b)	PO	Yes	5†	5	4x††	Markets with *buyer* market power are unable to overcome the institutional asymmetry, prices converge to the competitive levels.	99%
Holt and Davis (1990)	PO with Non-Binding Price Notices	Yes	3	*	2x	After early success at raising price above the pre-notice level (but not to the shared monopoly level), coordination breaks down and price converges to the pre-notice level.	NR
Davis and Holt (1991)	PO	No	either 3 or 5	*	12x	Supracompetitive prices are sustained throughout all the market power trials. However, the elevated prices seem to be due to tacit collusion rather than the exercise of market power.	NR
Davis and Williams (1991)	PO	Yes	5†	5(*)	4, 4x	Prices exceed CE price in all of the market trials with market power and simulated buyers. However, it is not clear whether market power is exercised, for the firms that structurally possess market power do not withhold units from the market. With human buyers, the market performance is more competitive.	91%* 92%

CE Competitive Equilibrium; DA Double-Auction; PO Posted-Offer; NR Not Reported; * Simulated buyers, and sellers have full information on the demand curve; x Trials in which participants have prior experience with the institution; † This uses the Holt, Langan, and Villamil (1986) design in which two sellers have substantially greater power than the other three sellers; and †† Four market power trials are summarized with the Davis and Williams (1991) experiments.

Table 4

Experimental Design

Cournot Homogeneous Product Mergers

	I	II
Premerger	5 firms (each with 20% of industry capital) **HHI = 2000**	11 firms (3 with 15%, 3 with 10%, and 5 with 5% of industry capital) **HHI = 1100**
Postmerger	4 firms (1 with 40%, and 3 with 20% of industry capital) **HHI = 2800**	10 firms (3 with 15%, 4 with 10%, and 3 with 5% of industry capital) **HHI = 1150**

SAMPLE DOUBLE-AUCTION INSTRUCTIONS

General

This is an experiment in the economics of market decisionmaking. The instructions are simple and if you follow them carefully and make good decisions you can earn money which will be paid to you in cash at the end of the experiment.

In this experiment we are going to conduct a market in which some of you will be buyers and some of you will be sellers in a sequence of market days or trading periods. Attached to the instructions you will find a sheet labeled Buyer or Seller, which describes to you the value of any decisions you might make. **You are not to reveal this information to anyone.** It is your own private information.

Specific Instructions to Buyers

During each market period you are free to purchase units from any seller or sellers. The first unit that you buy *during a trading period* you will receive the amount listed under unit 1 marked redemption value; if you buy a second unit you will receive the additional amount marked unit 2 redemption value. The profits from each purchase are computed by taking the difference between the redemption value and purchase price of the unit bought. That is,

your earnings = (redemption value) - (purchase price).

Suppose, for example, that you buy two units and that your redemption value for the first unit is 200 and for the second unit is 180. If you pay 150 for your first unit and 160 for your second unit, your earnings are:

earnings from first unit = 200 - 150 = 50

earnings from second unit = 180 - 160 = 20

total earnings = 50 + 20 = 70.

The blanks on the table will help you record your profits. The purchase price of the first unit that you buy during the first period should be recorded on your sheet *at the time of purchase.* You should then record your profit for that unit. At the end of the period record your total of profits for the period in the space provided. Subsequent periods should be recorded similarly.

Specific Instructions to Sellers

During each market period you are free to sell units to any buyer or buyers. The first unit that you sell *during a trading period* you obtain at a cost of the amount listed under unit 1 marked cost; if you sell a second unit you incur the cost listed for unit 2. Your profits from each sale are computed by taking the difference between the sales price of the unit and its cost. That is,

your earnings = (sales price of unit) - (cost of unit).

Suppose, for example, that you sell two units and that your cost of the first unit is 140 and of the second unit is 160. If you sell the first unit at 200 and the second unit at 190, your earnings are:

earnings from first unit = 200 - 140 = 60

earnings from second unit = 190 - 160 = 30

total earnings = 60 + 30 = 90.

The blanks on the table will help you record your profits. The sales price of the first unit you sell during the first period should be recorded on your sheet *at the time of purchase*. You should then record your profit for that unit. At the end of the period record the total of profits in the space provided. Subsequent periods should be recorded similarly.

Market Organization

The market for units is organized as follows. The trading period is open for **5 minutes**. Any buyer is free to bid and any seller is free to offer at any time that recognition is gained from the auctioneer. The bid (offer) is tendered by giving the sequence: name and bid price (offer price). For example, "buyer 7 bids 120" or "seller 6 offers 210." Recognized bids and offers are written on the board and will remain there until accepted, canceled or replaced by a higher (lower) bid (offer). Anyone is free to accept a standing bid (offer). For example, "seller 6 accepts buyer 7's bid of 120" or "buyer 7 accepts seller 6's offer of 210." Once a bid (offer) is accepted, a binding contract has been closed and both parties record the transaction. Completed transactions will be circled on the board.

Things to note

Always buy (sell) units in order of unit number.

You can only buy (sell) as many units as you have values (costs).

There is no carryover of untraded units across market periods.

SAMPLE RECORD TABLE
SELLER # __2__

PERIOD 1		UNIT 1	UNIT 2	UNIT 3	
	(A) Cost	4.00	4.70	4.75	
	(B) Sales Price				
	(C) Profit per unit [(B) - (A)]				
	(D) Profit this period				
	(E) Cumulative Profit				

PERIOD 2		UNIT 1	UNIT 2	UNIT 3	
	(A) Cost	4.00	4.70	4.85	
	(B) Sales Price				
	(C) Profit per unit [(B) - (A)]				
	(D) Profit this period				
	(E) Cumulative Profit				

PERIOD 3		UNIT 1	UNIT 2	UNIT 3	
	(A) Cost	4.00	4.70	4.85	
	(B) Sales Price				
	(C) Profit per unit [(B) - (A)]				
	(D) Profit this period				
	(E) Cumulative Profit				

PERIOD 4		UNIT 1	UNIT 2	UNIT 3	
	(A) Cost	4.00	4.70	4.85	
	(B) Sales Price				
	(C) Profit per unit [(B) - (A)]				
	(D) Profit this period				
	(E) Cumulative Profit				